Enameling on Metal Clay

Enameling on Metal Clay

INNOVATIVE JEWELRY PROJECTS

Pam East

Printed in the United States of America

11 10 09 08 07   1 2 3 4 5

The written instructions, photographs, designs,
and projects presented are intended for the personal use of the reader and may be reproduced
for that purpose only. Any other use, including
commercial use, is forbidden under law without
written permission of the copyright holder.

Please follow appropriate health and safety
measures when working with torches, kilns, and
enamels. Some general guidelines are presented
in this book, but always read and follow the
manufacturer's instructions.

Every effort has been made to ensure the
accuracy of the information presented; however,
the publisher is not responsible for any injuries,
losses, or other damages that may result from
the use of the information in this book.

These trademarks are used in an editorial fashion
only, without permission of the holders: Badger
Balm™, Crock-Pot®, The Enamelist Society™,
Klyr-Fire®, Soft Touch™, Sunshine® Polishing
Cloth, Teflon™, Teflex™, Tri-M-Ite®

Publisher's Cataloging-in-Publication Data
(Prepared by The Donohue Group, Inc.)

East, Pam.
   Enameling on metal clay : innovative jewelry
projects / Pam East.
    p. : ill. ; cm.
   ISBN: 978-0-87116-245-8
1. Enamel and enameling. 2. Precious metal clay.
3. Jewelry making.
I. Title.

TT382.6 .E27 2007
739.275

Introduction   6

Getting started   8

Metal clay supplies and tool kits   10
Enamel tool kits   14
Firing tools and equipment   16
Metal clay basics   20
Enamel basics   32

Projects   46

Quick & Easy Earrings   48
Introduction to basic techniques

Kaleidoscope Fantasy   54
Reversible pendant with leaded enamels

Golden Days of Summer   58
Sifted pendant with gold-foil accents

Awesome Blossoms   62
Pin with enamel floral wafers and threads

Let's Go Fly a Kite!   68
Syringe-work cloisonné pendant

Blue Horizon   72
Three-dimensional enamel ring

Here Kitty Kitty!   76
Paper-punch champlevé pendant

Bayou Bracelet   82
Torch-fired basse-taille beads

Gallery   88

Troubleshooting appendix   92

Resources   94

About the author   95

introduction

Simply put, enameling is the art of applying glass to metal.
For more than two thousand years, artisans have given their work
extra dimension and excitement by bonding thin layers of richly
colored glass to the surface of metal. Ancient examples exist today,
the color still as vibrant as the day it was made. And now metal clay
makes it possible to create beautiful jewelry with rich, lasting color
right in your own home or studio.

The first time you fire a piece of metal clay and watch the silver
emerge is a magical moment. The first time I did it, I felt like running
up to strangers on the street and shouting, "Look! I made this!"
Puzzled strangers notwithstanding, the fact that I could create
jewelry pieces in fine silver, without traditional metalsmithing skills,
was a revelation to me.

What drew me to metal clay is probably a little different than for
most people. I'm an enamelist, and for me, color is what it's all about.
I had been working on copper for several years, but was ready to
branch out into silver when metal clay opened the door for me.

As it turns out, metal clay has several advantages over traditional
metalsmithing for craft artisans like me. Aside from being able to
produce beautiful jewelry without thousands of dollars worth of
expensive equipment and years of training, the fact that metal
clay fires to 99.9% pure fine silver is a huge boon for an enamelist.
Most of the silver used in jewelry is sterling, which contains copper
and cannot be directly enameled. It must go through an involved
process called depletion gilding, which removes all the copper from
the surface, before it can be successfully enameled. By contrast,
fine silver – which metal clay is after firing – is ready for enameling
pretty much right out of the gate.

These exciting new ways of combining silver and enamel are just too good not to share, and I love to teach. My goal as a teacher has always been bridging the gap between home hobbyists and jewelry techniques commonly perceived as being too difficult or expensive. Often, with a little creativity and an openness to new materials and ideas, it turns out anyone can produce beautiful jewelry. I find nothing so exciting as seeing someone's face light up when she makes a piece of jewelry she thought was completely out of her reach, realizing she really can do it!

These exciting new ways of combining silver and enamel are just too good not to share.

For me, the only drawback to teaching is the limit to the number of people with whom I can share these wonderful new techniques. I knew I'd have to write a book to reach a wider audience. There are any number of fine-art enameling books already on the market and, while they are excellent, they can often be intimidating for the first-time enamelist. They also do not address the unique potential metal clay has with enamels.

My goal with this book is to give courage to those with little or no experience but who have the desire to explore something new. Try enameling on metal clay. Go for it! It's easy. And while you are busy with the techniques and projects in this book, expanding and exploring your own creativity, rest assured I'll be busy in my studio coming up with new things for you to try. Enameling on metal clay is such an endlessly varied experience, I know I'll never tire of this fantastically versatile combination. I'm betting neither will you.

– Pam East

Getting Started
Materials, tools, basic techniques

Consider this section your bible for enameling on metal clay!
Check the lists as you gather your tools for each project; to
keep the project lists simple, I refer you back to tool kits shown
in these pages. In this section you'll also find comprehensive
instructions for working with metal clay, enamel, kilns, torches,
and more.

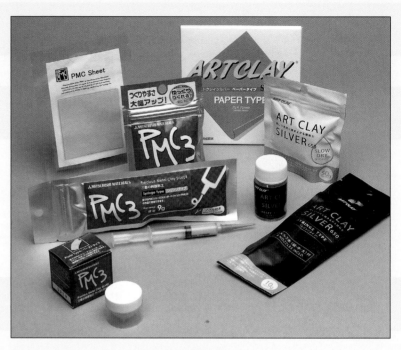

Metal clay supplies

For the projects in this book, you'll always start with a package of basic clay (sometimes referred to as "lump" clay).

There are two brands of metal clay on the market: **Art Clay Silver** (ACS), made by Aida Chemical, and **Precious Metal Clay** (PMC), made by Mitsubishi. Both types of clay are made of tiny particles of fine silver suspended in an organic binder. In its moist state, the clay can be rolled, molded, sculpted, stamped, and more. It is then dried and fired. Firing burns away the binder, leaving 99.9% fine silver.

Both ACS and PMC have a variety of clay formulas available. For the projects in this book, I recommend using **ACS 650 Low Fire** (Regular or Slow Dry), **PMC+**, or **PMC3**. I prefer ACS 650 Low Fire Slow Dry because it remains workable longer and shrinks less than the regular formula; however, with either ACS or PMC you will be able to produce lovely silver pieces suitable for enameling. Most of the projects in this book call for 10g to 20g of clay.

Metal clay comes in several other forms as well. ACS and PMC offer **paste, syringe, and paper** types. Paste, or "slip," as it is sometimes called, is a semi-liquid used for joining clay pieces and filling shallow cracks. Syringe clay has a consistency like cake frosting and is used for surface embellishments and designs. Syringe can also be used for repairs, joining clay pieces, and filling deep cracks. Paper or sheet-type metal clay is a thin, flexible sheet that can be folded, stamped, or cut into shapes.

There are a series of stages when working with metal clay. You will be working with wet clay, dry clay (which I refer to as greenware), and fired silver. I have divided the tool lists into these groupings to help you figure out what's needed at each stage.

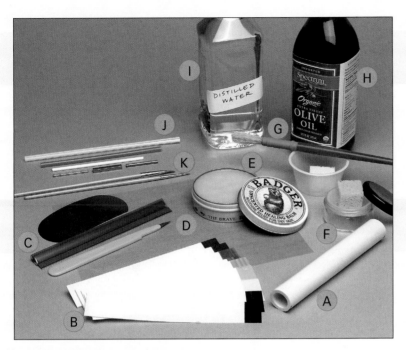

Wet clay tools

Working with moist silver clay is pretty much like working with any other kind of clay – you'll use tools to roll it, cut it, and shape it.

Use a **roller** to roll the clay to a desired thickness. You'll find acrylic rollers in craft stores in the polymer clay section, but it's less expensive and just as effective to cut a length of small-diameter PVC pipe for this purpose. **Graduated slats** help maintain an even thickness when rolling out metal clay. The color-coded slats come in six different thicknesses ranging from .25mm to 2mm (see chart on p. 22).

Flexible, reusable Teflon, Teflex, and similar **nonstick sheets** are ideal for working with wet or moist clay and can be cut into small sections or strips. **Badger Balm and olive oil** are natural, nonpetroleum lubricants that burn off clean when a metal clay piece is fired. Use on hands, tools, and textures to prevent the clay from sticking. A **stencil brush** is great for applying olive oil to textures and stamps. Soak a small piece of sponge in oil and use it to apply the oil to your brush for a very controlled application.

Buy **fine paintbrushes** with synthetic golden taklon bristles no more than ½-in. (13mm) long. My favorite sizes are liners or rounds in sizes #10/0, #1, and #2, and flat sizes #2 and #4. Keep a damp sponge handy for cleaning off your brushes as you work.

Unused clay needs to be stored in an airtight container so it doesn't dry out. Wrap your unused clay tightly in **plastic wrap** and tuck it into a **clay keeper**. The top is fitted with an insert for a damp sponge. As long as the sponge does not dry out and the keeper remains tightly closed, you can keep your clay moist and ready to use for long periods of time.

Although **distilled water** may not be strictly necessary, it will ensure you are not introducing contaminants into your metal clay and enamel.

Wet clay tool kit
- ❑ acrylic roller [A]
- ❑ graduated slats [B]
- ❑ cutting tools: cutter/scraper, tissue blade, scalpel [C]
- ❑ nonstick flexible work surface [D]
- ❑ Badger Balm [E]
- ❑ clay keeper [F]
- ❑ stencil brush, cup, sponge [G]
- ❑ olive oil [H]
- ❑ distilled water [I]
- ❑ straws and other hole cutters [J]
- ❑ fine paintbrushes [K]
- ❑ plastic wrap (not pictured)

The items listed here represent what I consider a minimum tool kit. Enjoy experimenting and adding more tools as you progress.

Greenware tool kit

- ❑ tidy tray [A]
- ❑ rubber block [B]
- ❑ sponge-backed sanding pads or sandpaper [C]
- ❑ small needle files [D]
- ❑ sanding swabs [E]
- ❑ sponge-tip applicator [F]
- ❑ carving tool [G]
- ❑ magnifying visor [H]

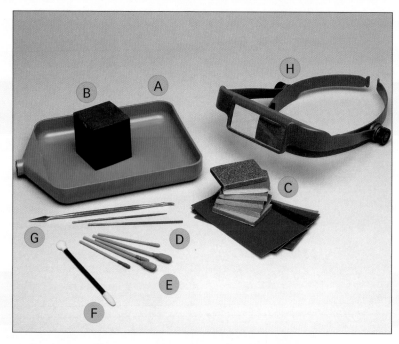

Greenware finishing tools

I use the term "greenware" to refer to the stage before firing where a metal clay piece is completely dry and safe to sand. This is a very important stage of the metal clay process. The better a job you do with your greenware, the more refined your finished piece will be. Having the right tools for the job is essential.

All the dust that comes off your piece as you sand it is made up of metal clay and can be recycled. By working over a **tidy tray**, you can easily capture all the dust and brush it into a jar for later use. Just add distilled water to make paste. The **rubber block** (2 in./5cm square) provides a raised, nonslip work surface that holds your piece steady over the tray.

For smoothing greenware I prefer working with **sponge-backed sanding pads**, but regular **sandpaper** will work as well. In either case, you need a variety of grits. For sandpaper, look for grits ranging from 400 to 2000 (the higher the number, the finer the grit). The sponge-backed sanding pads come in sets with grits ranging from 180 all the way up to 12,000. These super-high-grit sanding tools will begin to polish your piece before you even fire it, and are invaluable for getting a true mirror finish on your work. (For more on mirror finishing, see p. 30.)

Small needle files, sanding swabs, a sponge-tip applicator, and carving tools are useful for cleanup in hard-to-reach areas and for carving and shaping. A damp sponge-tip applicator is very handy for smoothing away small scratches and imperfections.

Wear a **magnifying visor** and check your piece thoroughly at the greenware stage, smoothing any flaws you find. Good magnification will allow you to catch these problems before firing, while they're still easy to fix.

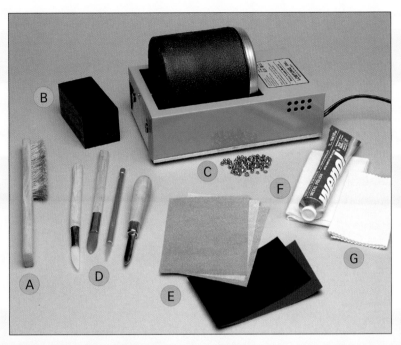

Silver finishing tool kit

❏ soft brass-wire brush [A]
❏ long rubber block [B]
❏ tumbler with stainless steel shot [C]
   and burnishing compound
   (not pictured)
❏ hand-burnishing tools [D]
❏ polishing papers and wet/dry
   sandpaper [E]
❏ metal polish and cloth [F]
❏ treated polishing cloth [G]

Silver finishing tools

Wire brushing is the first step in postfire finishing. Brushes come in steel or brass. I prefer a **soft brass-wire brush.**

A **rubber block** gives you a raised, nonslip work surface for polishing your work. I like using a long block (4 x 2 in./10 x 5cm) for polishing as it allows for longer strokes.

Tri-M-Ite polishing papers and wet/dry sandpaper are a must for achieving a high shine on your finished silver. When choosing sandpaper, be sure to look for the wet/dry variety, because much of your sanding will be done wet. Get a range of grits from 400 to 2000. Tri-M-Ite papers also can be used wet or dry and go all the way to 8000 grit, which is helpful for achieving a mirror finish.

Hand burnishers come in a variety of styles. A metal burnisher is effective and inexpensive. I prefer agate burnishers as I find they are less likely to scratch your work and are super smooth. They are a bit more expensive, but worth it. The agate ball tip is great for getting into hard-to-reach places.

Tumble-polishing with a **tumbler, stainless steel shot, water, and a burnishing compound** is by far the easiest and most thorough method of burnishing your silver in preparation for enameling. Mixed shot gives good results, reaching all the surfaces of the silver to harden and polish.

Buffing with **metal polish and a cloth** is the final step in polishing your work. **Sunshine cloth** is pretreated with polish and does not require application of metal polish. Use these only after enameling because polishes can discolor enamel.

Enamel prep tool kit
❏ 200-mesh screen with coin [A]
❏ recycled office paper [B]
❏ plastic cups [C]
❏ plastic spoons [D]
❏ plastic pipettes [E]
❏ distilled water [F]
❏ dust mask (N95 or N100) [G]

Silver prep tool kit
❏ clear ammonia [H]
❏ glass brushes [I]
❏ latex or rubber gloves [J]

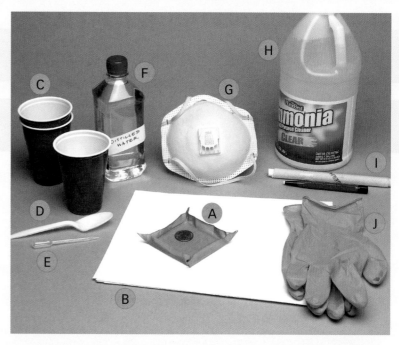

Enamel/silver preparation tools

As with metal clay, enameling falls into groups of activities, and I have divided the tool lists accordingly. For enameling, these activities are **preparation, application** (wet-pack or sifting), **firing, and finishing**.

Preparing enamels sometimes requires prescreening. Use a 200-mesh **enamel screen**. A **clean coin** (a quarter is a good size) is helpful for pushing the enamel through the screen. Work over **paper** so you can reclaim the enamel sifted out. This is a good use for recycled office paper.

Have a good supply of **plastic cups, plastic spoons, and pipettes** for washing your enamels or working with them wet. As with metal clay, using **distilled water** will prevent contamination by unwanted minerals or other substances.

A **good dust mask** (N95 or N100) is necessary whenever you screen or sift your enamels (see *Health and Safety*, p. 19).

You will need to clean your silver with **ammonia and a glass brush** prior to enameling. Use only clear ammonia – never scented or sudsing types. Wear **latex or rubber gloves** to avoid getting glass fibers in your fingers.

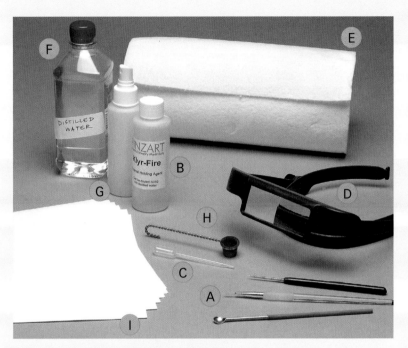

Wet-pack tool kit
- ❏ application tools: small enamel spoon, fine paintbrush, scribe [A]
- ❏ Klyr-Fire enamel adhesive [B]
- ❏ plastic pipette [C]
- ❏ magnifying visor [D]
- ❏ paper towels [E]
- ❏ distilled water [F]

Sifting tool kit
- ❏ fine paintbrush [A]
- ❏ Klyr-Fire enamel adhesive [B]
- ❏ magnifying visor [D]
- ❏ distilled water [F]
- ❏ spray bottle [G]
- ❏ ½-in. (13mm) sifter [H]
- ❏ recycled office paper [I]

Wet-pack and sifting tools

Wet-packing and **sifting** are two methods for applying enamels to silver. Although many of the necessary tools are common to both methods, some are specific. Even if you find you strongly prefer one method of application over another, it's a good idea to have tools for both on hand.

To wet-pack, you'll use a **small enamel spoon, fine paintbrushes, and a scribe**. The tiny spoon is great for measuring out small amounts of enamel and mixing it with water. Get golden taklon round or liner brushes in sizes #10/0 and #1 with bristles no more than ½ in. (13mm) long. A scribe or other pointed tool assists in positioning the grains of enamel.

Klyr-Fire enamel adhesive is used full strength for some wet-packing applications such as counter-enameling and on three-dimensional pieces where the enamel must stay in place on an angle. A **plastic pipette** or eyedropper is useful for adding water and Klyr-Fire to enamel.

For sifted applications, you will need to dilute Klyr-Fire 1:1 with **distilled water** and put it in a **sprayer**. Mist it onto the piece to keep sifted enamels in place until you fire them. **Sifters** come in a variety of sizes. For jewelry projects, a ½-in. (13mm) sifter will be sufficient.

Enamel finishing tools

For enamel finishing, you'll use the same tool kit as you do for silver finishing (see p. 13), with the addition of one important tool: an **alundum stone**. Use this stone to grind off stray enamel.

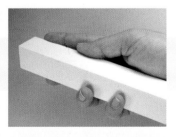

Firing tools

A small butane torch [A], like those used for making crème brulee, is popular for firing metal clay pieces because it's inexpensive and easy to find. Although you can fire the metal clay part of many projects this way, you will not be able to use a butane torch for the enamel step.

Kilns range in price and features, from a small, beehive-style kiln to a high-end, fully programmable kiln like those made by Paragon and Sierra.

The UltraLite kiln [B] is far less expensive than a full-size kiln and it can handle most, if not all, metal clay and enameling tasks. The working area is just 3 in. (76mm) across, which is big enough for most jewelry pieces. Weighing just two pounds, it can sit on your work table and you can pop things in and out of it without having to get up.

The Paragon model SC-2 [C] is an excellent example of a programmable kiln and I highly recommend it. It is available with an optional window (not shown), which is perfect for enameling because you need to keep a close eye on the fusing process. The kiln is easy to operate and takes all the guesswork out of both processes – firing the metal clay and applying the enamels. It operates on normal household current.

Most of the projects in this book require kiln firing. If you're not ready to invest in a kiln and would like to try these projects, contact your local college or university art department to see if they have firing available or can direct you to firing services. Some cities have studios with kilns that can be rented by the hour. Enamelist clubs also may be able to help (see *Resources,* p. 94).

Firing equipment

There are two stages to firing all the projects in this book. First you'll fire the metal clay to burn out the organic binder and prepare it for enameling. Second, after applying the enamel, you'll fire again to fuse the enamel onto the metal clay.

For the first step, firing the metal clay piece, you have several options – torch-firing with a small **butane torch**, firing in a **lightweight economy kiln**, or using a large **programmable kiln**.

For the second firing, which fuses the enamel to the metal clay piece, I recommend that you use some type of kiln to give you the control you need for this step. (The exceptions are the first project, where I'll demonstrate how you can fire small pieces over a gas stovetop, and the last project, where we'll use a propane torch to fuse the enamel.)

In each project, I've listed the firing equipment that's appropriate for each of the two firing stages of the projects. You can decide which method you'd like to use.

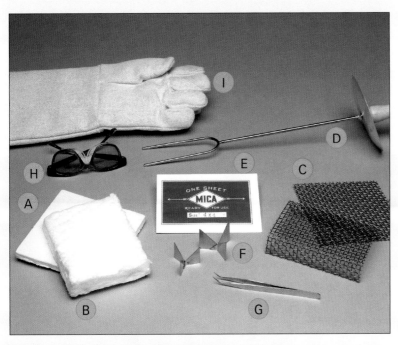

Programmable kiln tool kit
❏ **kiln shelf [A]**
❏ **fiber blanket [B]**
❏ **firing rack [C]**
❏ **firing fork [D]**
❏ **sheet mica [E]**
❏ **trivets [F]**
❏ **long bentnose tweezers [G]**
❏ **green IR filter safety glasses [H]**
❏ **heat-resistant gloves [I]**

Programmable kiln tools

Firing with a programmable kiln requires a number of specialized tools. The main challenge with kiln firing is getting items that are extremely hot in and out of the kiln safely, and that is what the majority of these tools do.

Metal clay items can be set directly on the **kiln shelf** for firing. Some three-dimensional items can be nested on a **fiber blanket** to help maintain the shape during firing.

A **firing rack** is used in enameling for taking items in and out of the kiln. The rack comes flat; bend two edges down with a vise or pliers to form a raised table. Use a **firing fork** to move the firing rack in and out of the kiln.

Place enameled items on a **sheet of mica** or a **trivet** rather than directly on the firing rack to protect them from marks, discoloration, or contamination. **Long bentnose tweezers** are helpful for moving hot items on and off the kiln shelves, firing racks, and trivets.

See *Health and safety*, p. 19, for **safety items** to have on hand when firing.

UltraLite kiln tool kit
- ❏ UltraLite electric kiln [A]
- ❏ ceramic inserts [B]
- ❏ small spatula [C]
- ❏ long bentnose tweezers [D]
- ❏ low-profile trivet [E]
- ❏ sheet mica [F]

Stovetop firing tool kit
- ❏ steel wire firing screen [G]
- ❏ long bentnose tweezers [D]
- ❏ firing rack [H]

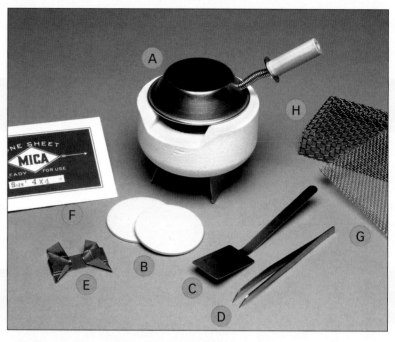

UltraLite firing tools

UltraLite and stovetop firing do not require much in the way of additional tools, and what you do need is relatively inexpensive. These are both very economical ways to get started enameling on metal clay.

For UltraLite firing: The optional **ceramic inserts** help retain heat. Set one inside the unit when firing metal clay.

Use **a small spatula and long bentnose tweezers** to move items in and out of the UltraLite. The spatula is included with the unit.

A trivet is needed for counter-enameling. You can use **sheet mica** to hold your piece when there is no counter-enamel.

Gas stovetop firing tools

Your items to be fired will go on the **steel wire firing screen**, and the screen will be placed on the burner during firing.

Use **long bentnose tweezers** to move items on and off the firing screen. Hot items can be placed on a **firing rack** to cool after they are fired.

health and safety

Working with enamels, kilns, and torches can be hazardous. Please be sure to read all instructions for the various tools, chemicals, and materials you will be using, including the Material Safety Data Sheets (MSDS). Use appropriate safety equipment where needed.

The tips listed here are just an overview, designed to help you avoid the most common missteps. They are in no way complete or comprehensive. If you are seriously injured, seek medical attention. The most important safety tool is the one between your ears. Use common sense!

Protect your eyes

Wear filtered protective glasses when looking into a kiln. The heat from kilns produces Infrared Radiation (IR), which is bad for your eyes over the long term. Look for green glass safety glasses intended for filtering IR.

Working with heat

Whenever you are working with kilns and torches there is the very real danger of burns and fires. Always keep a fire extinguisher nearby. Use heat-resistant gloves when taking items in and out of the kiln.

Enamel handling

Enamel is powdered glass and can be very irritating to your nose, throat, and lungs. Wear at least an N95 or N100 dust mask whenever you are sifting enamels. Wash your hands often. Never lick your wet-pack or other enamel handling tools. Do not eat, drink, or smoke in your work area. Do not sweep or vacuum unless you have a special filter that will capture all your enamel dust; use a wet mop or wipe down with water instead. Work in a well-ventilated area when firing enamels.

When firing leaded enamel, there is the possibility that harmful vapors will be released. Do not torch-fire or stovetop-fire leaded enamels. Take care not to over-fire them. Vent your kiln during firing. This means removing the vent plug that fits in the top of most kilns. It's best to have an active ventilation system near your kiln as well. If you do not have an exhaust hood, set a box fan to blow out a window.

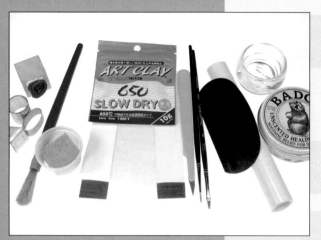

Because metal clay has a short working time, assemble all your tools before you open the package.

A light coating of olive oil will prevent clay from sticking in the texture stamp. Use a stencil brush, a condiment cup, and a small sponge soaked in olive oil.

A light tap into the oil with the brush is all you need.

Preparing your work space

Metal clay begins to dry the moment you open the package, so efficiency is important. You don't want to waste time looking for your tools after your clay is open, so have your tools ready and your work space prepared. It's helpful to mentally walk through the steps to be sure you have everything you need. Review *Wet clay tools* on p. 11 for a typical list. Also check the specialty tools for the specific project you've chosen.

If you are using a heated device for drying your clay, turn it on before you begin so it can begin to warm up.

Lightly coat your hands with Badger Balm or olive oil. Go easy! You don't want to be oily or greasy; you want just a thin barrier that will prevent your hands from pulling the moisture out of the clay and will keep the clay from sticking to your fingers.

Use what's on your hands to lightly coat your roller and your work surface. It doesn't take much. You want just a very light coating so the clay doesn't stick. You shouldn't see streaks of oil or balm. A little bit goes a long way.

If you are using a texture or stamp, you will need to give it a very light coating of olive oil. Forgetting this step will lead to a very unhappy half hour or so picking clay out of your stamp. Soak a sponge in olive oil and place it in a condiment cup for easy access. Tap a stencil brush on the oily sponge and then tap and brush it into your texture. This method puts on just the barest coating. The oil should not pool in the texture.

Is everything in place? Now you're ready to open your clay and begin!

Working with wet clay

When working with metal clay, a good rule of thumb is the "10-80-10 plan." This means plan to spend 10% of your time working with the wet clay, 80% of your time on greenware sanding and finishing, and 10% of your time on postfire finishing. Don't get too caught up in trying to get it "perfect" in the wet clay stage. You'll have plenty of time for refining and perfecting after it's in the dry greenware stage.

Have a plan in mind before you begin. It's sometimes helpful to create a model in polymer clay first, so you've already practiced the steps. Polymer clay is also useful for testing textures and stamps to see what they will look like in the clay. If working time is an issue for you, try Art Clay Silver 650 Slow Dry clay.

Keep plastic wrap and a clay keeper on hand while you're working. Wrap up any scraps as you trim them off to keep them from drying out.

Don't fight with a piece that's drying out and cracking. It takes less time to make a piece over at this stage than to fill and repair all the cracks and problems later on. Give it a spray of distilled water, wad it up, and wrap it up in plastic wrap. Wait 5 or 10 minutes for it to rehydrate and start over. Because you will have practiced, it will probably go better the second time around anyway.

Use a piece of scrap polymer clay to test the look of a texture.

21

tip

When working on complex projects, it's helpful to create a model in polymer clay before using metal clay. A slightly rounded ¼ teaspoon of polymer clay is equivalent in volume to 10 grams of metal clay. A slightly rounded ½ teaspoon is equivalent to 20 grams of metal clay.

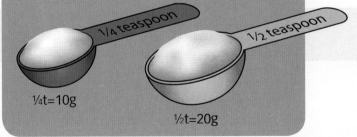

¼t=10g

½t=20g

slat color	inch	mm	cards
	.01"	0.25	1
	.02"	0.50	2
	.03"	0.75	3
	.04"	1.00	4
	.06"	1.50	6
	.08"	2.00	8

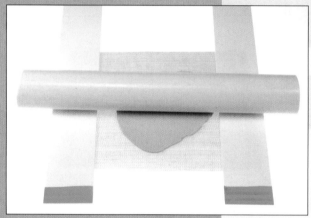

Work on a nonstick surface and roll the clay out from the center.

Rolling clay

There are a variety of ways to roll out metal clay. The most common is to keep the ends of the roller on raised surfaces, with the clay between. Many people use playing cards for this purpose, but I prefer a plastic graduated slat set. The slats are long and narrow and will give consistent results over time. They are color coded by thickness. The chart shown here lists the colors and thickness in millimeters, inches, and playing card equivalents. Throughout this book I will refer to which color slat to use for each project. If you prefer to use cards, you can use this chart to determine the playing card equivalent.

For this technique you will need a graduated slat set, a roller, and a Teflex-type sheet or other nonstick work surface.

Place the slats on your nonstick work surface far enough apart to make room for your clay to be rolled out, but still close enough together so the roller rests on them. If you are rolling out on a texture, it's best if you can place the slats directly on the texture sheet. If you have to place the slats off the texture, you may need to use a slightly thicker slat, or stack additional slats, to add a bit more height.

Place your clay between the slats. Place the roller in the middle of the clay, with the ends positioned over the slats and begin rolling it back and forth, working out from the center. If you need to roll the clay in a different direction, pick up the clay and turn it rather than moving the slats or the roller. Continue rolling out the clay until the roller rests on the slats and the clay is an even thickness, the same height as your chosen slat. Changing direction on a texture is not recommended.

Drying clay

Dry your metal clay pieces completely before sanding and firing. (If there is any moisture in the clay when you fire it, the piece could bubble or explode.) If you are air-drying it, give it a minimum of 24 hours drying time before firing.

You can speed the process along with low heat. A hot plate, cup warmer, or a toaster oven set to 150°F (66°C) will work. You can also use a food dehydrator to speed things along. Although metal clay is nontoxic, once you use an item with metal clay, it's good practice not to use it with food.

With the addition of low heat, the clay will take anywhere from 30 minutes to an hour to dry, depending on the clay formula, the size and thickness of your piece, and how you're drying it.

Here's an easy test for dryness. Take the warm piece out of the dryer and place it on a mirror or a reflective tool like a clay scraper. Wait a few seconds and then move it aside. If you see condensation on the mirrored surface, the piece is not yet dry.

tip

Wet metal clay can be air dried, but you can speed it along with the use of a hair dryer, dehydrator, hot plate, toaster oven, or even a mug warmer.

Photo: *Art Jewelry* magazine

Greenware finishing

I use the term "greenware" – borrowed from ceramics – to refer to metal clay that is thoroughly dry but not yet fired. One of the characteristics of metal clay is that you are able to do the vast majority of the finish work before you fire it. The more time you put into a piece at the greenware stage, the less you'll have to do after you fire it.

The smoother a finish you get on your greenware, the finer a finish you will have on your silver after it is fired. Getting to that fine, smooth finish means sanding, sanding, and a little more sanding. Believe me, it's much easier to file and sand greenware than silver, so take your time and do it before firing.

One of my favorite tools is a sponge-backed sanding pad. These pads come in a variety of grits ranging from 180 to 12,000. When sanding with these pads or with regular sandpaper, which also works, work from coarse to fine. Lower numbers are coarser; higher numbers are finer. I rarely use the very coarse grits unless I'm trying to remove a big lump or bump, or completely reshaping the piece. I usually start with 400 grit.

Sand any area that should be smooth. (You don't want to sand away textures!) Hold the work close to the spot you are sanding to avoid breaking it. Look for rough spots around the edges and areas that should be flat. You can also smooth sharp corners, points, or edges at this point. Remember, this will be metal, so anything sharp will be uncomfortable to wear. You want to make jewelry, not weapons! When you finish one grit, move to the next-finer grit and begin again. Repeat this process all the way up to the finest grit you have. Greenware is easy to sand and smooth, so even though it sounds like a lot of work, it really goes very quickly.

Work over a tidy tray to collect all the dust being sanded off. This dust is metal clay and can later be rehydrated into paste. A rubber block in your tray provides a stable, nonslip area for bracing your work.

There are a number of ways to work on tight spots and interior spaces. A good set of mini needle files will serve you well. In addition to smoothing out bail holes and other tight corners, you can also use them to carve and shape your greenware. For some enameling projects, they are indispensable for squaring off the sides of interior spaces to be enameled.

Another set of tools I like are sanding swabs. These little swabs are covered with the same sanding material as the sponge-backed sanding pads and are perfect for sanding and smoothing otherwise hard-to-get-to areas.

A good magnifying visor is essential for greenware finishing. Imperfections that are overlooked at this stage can become glaringly obvious after the piece is fired. You have a better chance of catching these with proper magnification and lighting.

I like to use sponge-backed sanding pads. Rest the piece on a rubber block in a tray so you can reclaim the clay dust.

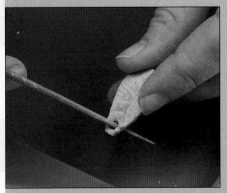

A good set of small needle files will come in handy for smoothing holes and other tight spots.

A damp sponge-tip applicator can help smooth out a problem area.

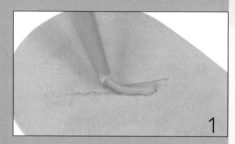

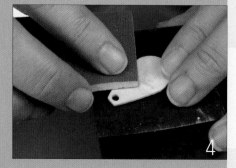

Repairing cracks and scratches

Sometimes small cracks, scratches, divots, or other uninten- tional impressions will appear in your greenware. Superficial imperfections are fairly easy to deal with. One of my favorite techniques is using a damp sponge-tip applicator to gently "erase" the problem. This works great, and is helpful for getting into tight spots. You also can use sandpaper to remove light scratches.

Deeper cracks will have to be filled. I like to use a metal clay syringe for this. Syringe clay has a consistency like cake frosting and is perfect for filling problem areas.

[1] Lay a line of syringe along area to be filled.

[2] Use a damp, flat brush (#2 or #4) to pat the syringe into place. If the syringe clay sticks to the brush, the brush isn't damp enough. If water pools on the piece, the brush is too damp. This just takes a little practice.

[3] Use the brush to gently smooth the line, working from the centerline out, rather than moving with the line. It's best to overfill the area slightly. As the syringe clay dries, it will settle in a bit.

[4] Sand the repair smooth.

If the problem is in a textured area, brush paste onto the piece, forcing the paste into the crack. Follow the texture with the brush. This should greatly reduce the appearance of the crack without covering up the texture. Generally speaking, small im- perfections in a heavily textured area aren't too noticeable, so don't worry if you can't make it disappear completely.

Repairing breaks

Remember, even the experts break things from time to time, so don't be too hard on yourself. When I was working on my Metal Clay Champlevé article for the September 2005 issue of *Art Jewelry* magazine, I dropped one of the pendants on the way to the kiln and it broke into eight pieces! I repaired the piece, fired it, and moved on. A reader would find it very difficult to tell which of the four pendants pictured was the one I broke. So sit back, take a deep breath, and relax. It's going to be fine.

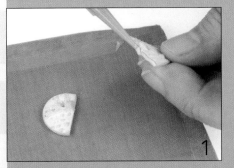

[1] Tape a piece of nonstick work surface to a piece of cardstock. (This platform allows you to move the repaired piece aside to dry without putting any stress on the repair joint.) Lay a line of syringe along one edge of the break.

[2] Gently press the pieces together, lining them up into their original positions. If you are working with very small pieces, a pair of tweezers, good lighting, and a magnifying visor will help a lot.

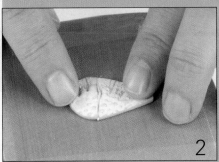

[3] The excess syringe clay may squeeze out of the joint. Use a damp brush to smooth it out. If the back of your piece is untextured don't worry about smoothing it out yet. You can fix it up after the repair is dry. If you have a texture to deal with, you can gently turn the piece over and smooth out the joint on that side too, but be careful not to break it apart again. It's better not to move the piece at all if you can avoid it.

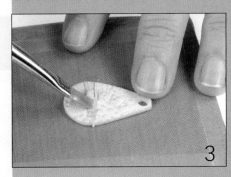

[4] When the repair is dry, examine it carefully under good light with a magnifying visor. The joint across the back will be very visible and you will need to reinforce it before attempting any sanding or smoothing. Use syringe to fill and conceal the repair. Treat it as you would a crack or scratch, overfilling it slightly and smoothing it from the centerline out with a flat brush.

[5] When the repair is dry, smooth it out as you normally would, but take care not to sand all the way back down to the seam.

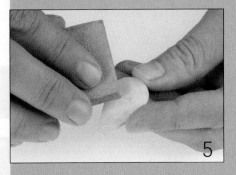

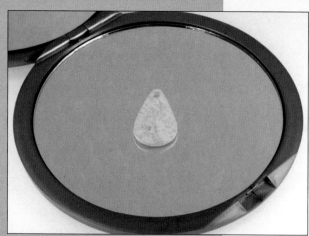

To check for dryness, place a warm piece on a mirror. If no condensation appears, it's dry and safe to fire. Don't keep your mirror on top of the dehydrator or other heated surface – condensation won't form on a warm mirror.

Firing metal clay

Metal clay must be completely dry before firing, or the piece could bubble or explode when fired. If air-drying, allow a minimum of 24 hours.

Metal clay firing schedules are determined by which clay product was used and what else was incorporated into the piece. To prepare metal clay for enameling, you should always fire it at the highest recommended temperature. Use the guide on this page for the projects in this book unless otherwise noted in the project chapter.

Those of you familiar with metal clay will note that this guide is slightly more aggressive than the manufacturer-suggested firing times and temperatures. Especially for enameling, it's important to fully fire the silver, reducing the porosity as much as possible. The additional time and/or temperature will not hurt the silver in any way and safeguards against underfiring the clay.

There are, of course, other clay formulas and schedules. For firing information on other metal clay products, see the manufacturer's instructions included with each package.

firing metal clay in a kiln

Kiln firing is the most reliable method, especially if you are using a programmable kiln.

The Orton Sentry Xpress 4.0 Controller is used to regulate many different models and brands of kilns. It can display the temperature in either Fahrenheit or Centigrade. A full instruction manual is included with the kiln, but the simple instructions on p. 27 should get you off to a quick start.

KILN FIRING	ramp speed	temperature	hold time
Art Clay Silver 650 *(Regular or Slow Dry)* or **PMC3**	Full	1500°F/815°C	10 min.
PMC+	Full	1650°F/900°C	15 min.
ULTRALITE FIRING			
Art Clay Silver 650 *(Regular or Slow Dry)* or **PMC3**	—	Full	20 min.
PMC+	—	Full	30 min.

controller settings for firing metal clay

[1] Press the **Start/Stop** button until the display reads **Pr0** or **SPd** followed by a number.

[2] Press the **HIGHER** button until you reach **SPd5**. This will alternate with **FULL**. If you scroll past **SPd5**, do not use the **LOWER** button. That will launch the program at this stage. Just continue using the **HIGHER** button until **SPd5** comes around again. This step sets the ramp speed (how quickly the kiln reaches the desired temperature). These instructions are for clay only, with no inclusions. Different ramp speeds may be necessary if other materials were incorporated into the clay piece.

[3] Press the **Start/Stop** button again to move to the next programming segment.

[4] °F **1** will display, alternating with the programmed temperature. Press the **HIGHER** or **LOWER** buttons until the display reaches the desired firing temperature.

[5] Press the **Start/Stop** button.

[6] **HLd1** will display, alternating with the set hold time. Press the **HIGHER** or **LOWER** buttons until the display reaches the desired hold time. Time is displayed in hours and minutes. For 10 minutes the display should read 00.10.

[7] Press the **Start/Stop** button two more times. The first time, **Strt** will display. The second time, **-ON-** will display. At this point, the kiln is on and firing will commence per your programmed instructions.

The unit will default to these settings until you change them, so the next time you can just use the **LOWER** button after reaching **SPd5** to review and launch that sequence.

To fire the clay, simply place it on a kiln shelf in the kiln and launch the program as described above. Once the program cycle is finished, the kiln will beep and shut off automatically. As long as you're firing just metal clay without inclusions, go ahead and open the kiln door to speed up the cooling time. You can use a pair of tweezers to remove the piece from the kiln to cool it faster. Be sure to wear heat-resistant gloves when you do this, and place the piece on a tile, extra kiln shelf, or some other surface that won't burn.

Don't quench the hot piece in water (see p. 28).

If you have a programmable kiln, chances are it's regulated by a Sentry Xpress controller such as this one.

The UltraLite kiln measures just 5½ in. (14cm) across and plugs into a standard 120V outlet.

Dim the lights during stovetop firing to help see when your piece reaches this salmon-pink color.

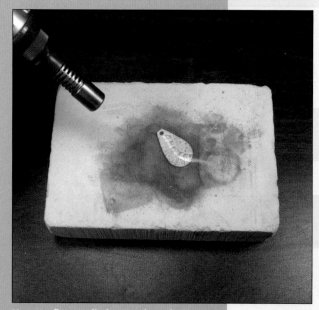

You can fire small pieces using a butane torch and a firing brick. This is the same kind of torch sold for kitchen use.

firing metal clay in an UltraLite

Starting an UltraLite is about as simple as it gets. Just plug it in! I recommend getting the ceramic inserts that are available as an accessory. Place an insert on the element. Place a second insert on top of the lid. This helps hold in the heat better, and also serves as a drying area. Put the lid on and preheat the unit for 35 minutes.

The top-end temperature for an UltraLite is just 1500°F (815°C), so the firing times need to be a bit longer than in a conventional kiln. Remove the lid and use tweezers or the spatula to place the piece on the ceramic insert in the UltraLite. Fire the piece with the lid off. A small amount of smoke will come off the piece as it begins to fire. This is just the binder burning off and is normal. Fire according to the schedule on p. 26. Remove the piece and allow it to air cool.

firing metal clay on a gas stovetop

This method should be used for ACS 650 and PMC3 only. Place a stainless steel wire mesh screen on your gas burner and turn the flame on high. Red hot spots will appear fairly quickly. Visually note where the hot spots are and turn off the burner. Use a pair of long bentnose tweezers to gently place your piece on the mesh over one of the hot spots. Turn the burner back on high. You will see a small amount of smoke and the piece may flame up for a few seconds. This is just the binder burning off and is normal. Wait for the piece to reach a light salmon-pink color and then begin timing for a minimum of 5 minutes. I recommend dimming the lights in your kitchen in order to see the color of the metal better. Once firing is complete, turn off the stove, but leave the piece in place to cool for at least 20 minutes.

firing metal clay with a torch

Pieces weighing 25 grams or less may be fired using a hand-held butane torch. Place the piece on a firing brick. Light your torch and begin sweeping the flame back and forth over the piece. You will see a small amount of smoke and the piece may flame up for a few seconds. Wait for the piece to reach a light salmon-pink color and then begin timing for 2 to 5 minutes. Again, dimming the lights will help tremendously. The larger or thicker your piece, the longer you should fire it. Use a timer, not a clock, to time the firing so you can keep your eyes on the color of the metal.

don't quench!

After firing, some people dip their work in water to cool it off fast. This is not something I recommend, especially for a piece that is going to be enameled. The super-rapid cooling may cause the piece to become more brittle, and water may get "steamed" into pores and crevices in the metal and come back later to haunt you when you are firing your enamel. Letting your piece air cool really doesn't take that long, and is worth the wait.

Postfire finishing

Metal clay, by nature, is somewhat porous. This can pose some additional challenges when it comes to enameling. Because of the pores, it's more prone to releasing silver salts into enamel, discoloring it. The problem can be alleviated somewhat by burnishing the piece after firing to compress the pores.

After the metal clay has been fired it appears white. In the photo to the right, you can see the difference in color and the shrinkage. Brushing the fired silver with a wire brush will begin to bring up the silver color you expect. Brush it vigorously with a brass wire brush using a mild soap or detergent and water. The soap and water will prevent any brass from transferring itself to the silver.

Now the piece needs to be burnished. The most efficient method is to use a tumbler loaded with stainless steel mixed shot, water, and a burnishing compound. The shot can easily get into little nooks and crannies that would be hard to access with a hand burnisher.

tumbling

Load the tumbler barrel with about a pound of mixed stainless steel shot. Add water until it is just half an inch or so above the shot. Add ½ teaspoon of burnishing compound. More is not better; use just the minimum amount recommended. Add your pieces and secure the lid of the tumbler per the manufacturer's directions. Set the barrel on the base and begin tumbling. For enameling, it's important that the work be very well burnished, so I recommend tumbling for at least 4 hours. I usually set up my tumbler before bedtime and let it run overnight.

hand burnishing

To hand burnish, simply rub the piece with the curved edge of the burnisher. I prefer using an agate burnisher rather than a metal one. Use a fair amount of pressure to shine the metal and close the pores. Take care not to catch the piece with the tip of the burnisher as this can scratch it. Try using a ball-tip burnisher to get into tight spaces and textures.

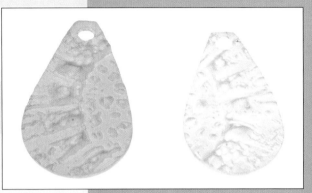

On the left is greenware; on the right is a piece after firing and before burnishing.

To bring up the silver color, brush with soapy water and a brass wire brush.

I prefer burnishing using a tumbler loaded with about a pound of shot, water, and burnishing compound.

If you don't have a tumbler, you can hand burnish your pieces. I like using an agate burnisher for this.

1

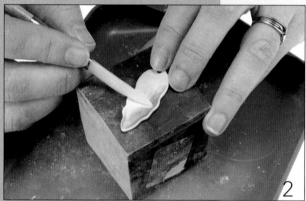

2

Mirror finishing

Now, I can hear you asking, "If tumbling will make my piece silvery and shiny, why go to the trouble of mirror finishing?" Good question! And truthfully, mirror finishing is not for everyone. If your piece is textured, there's not much point to it. But if your piece has smooth areas, you can really kick it up a notch with mirror finishing. The more finely you finish your work, the more professional and amazing it will look. There's nothing so impressive as gleaming, mirror-smooth silver! Once you see the difference between "shiny" and "mirror" for yourself, you'll understand what I mean. I challenge you to try it and see.

[1] Mirror finishing starts in the greenware stage. The smoother and more refined you get the greenware, the easier it will be to mirror finish after it's dry. Make good use of your sponge-backed sanding pads and other sanding tools, working your way from the coarser grits to the most fine. Examine the piece carefully using a magnifying visor to look for small scratches and divots. These may look minor at this stage but can prevent achieving a true mirror finish later on. Fill or sand out any problems now.

[2] As a final step before firing, use an agate burnisher to gently burnish the greenware smooth. This will give the smoothest finish possible, and will also highlight any scratches or divots you may have missed.

Shiny finish

Mirror finish

shiny vs. mirror finish

There is a subtle but distinct difference between a shiny finish and a mirror finish. A shiny finish will look like bright, shiny silver, but the surface may be irregular and no reflections can be seen in it. A mirror finish is perfectly smooth and free of divots or scratches. It will show a reflection of surrounding objects. Tumbling will definitely make your silver shiny, but only hand finishing can give it a true mirror finish.

[3] After the piece is fired, brush it with a soft brass wire brush. Use an agate burnisher to burnish the silver. This is an important step because burnishing compresses the metal and smooths over light surface imperfections.

[4] If there is enamel on the piece, all sanding must be done wet. If it's silver only, you can sand it either wet or dry. Start with 600-grit sandpaper, working in one direction. I recommend working on a 4-in. (10cm) rubber block. This helps prevent the piece from sliding around as you work. You should reach a point where only the uniform scratches from the 600-grit paper are visible. If you cannot get all the scratches out of the surface, it may be necessary to back up to 400 grit. Be sure to sand all sides and areas you want to be mirror finished.

[5] Rinse the piece and your rubber block. Using 1000-grit sandpaper, work at a 90º angle from the previous paper. You should be able to remove all signs of scratches from the previous grit.

[6] Switch to Tri-M-Ite polishing papers. Following the process above, work your way through green, gray, blue, pink, and mint, rinsing with water and switching the angle of sanding between each one.

[7] If you are not adding enamel to the piece, buff it vigorously with metal polish and a soft flannel polishing cloth. Do not polish a piece that will be enameled.

3

4

5

6

7

31

granular stage

orange-peel stage

glossy and smooth stage

What is enamel?

Enamel is richly colored glass that has been formulated to create a permanent bond with metals. It is manufactured by a number of companies in countries around the world, and is available in both leaded and lead-free formulas. For the vast majority of my enameling, I prefer to use Thompson medium-expansion, medium-temperature, lead-free enamels for copper, silver, and gold, which are produced in the United States.

To make enamel, glass is smelted, then poured out in sheets that are crushed and ground into powder. This powder is sifted through mesh screens to sort it by particle size. The most commonly produced size is 80 mesh. When purchasing 80-mesh enamel, you get everything that passes through a screen with 80 holes per linear inch. That means everything from the largest particle that will fit through the screen right down to the finest dust. This fine dust, called *fines,* can cause cloudiness in transparent enamels and can be removed before use (see *Preparing enamels,* p. 35).

Enamel goes through several stages as it fuses. First it reaches the granular stage, where it begins to stick to the metal but retains its characteristic grainy texture. Then it reaches the orange-peel stage, where it has started to smooth out but has some texture like the peel of an orange. Finally it reaches the glossy and smooth stage and is fully fused. Ideally, you want to fire the piece just until it reaches the final stage, but no longer. Overfiring the enamels can result in them darkening or discoloring, so watch the process closely.

enameling techniques

Of all the enamel application techniques, *cloisonné* is probably the most widely known. In traditional cloisonné, thin, flat wires are bent to create designs and then attached to a solid metal base. This creates cells, which are then filled with enamel. With metal clay, we use syringe clay in place of wires.

In *basse-taille,* a textured or patterned surface is completely covered with transparent enamels. The pattern or texture is visible beneath the enamels, giving lovely variations to the color.

In *champlevé* enameling, designs are impressed into the piece and then filled to the top with enamel. In traditional metalsmithing, the texture of basse-taille and the impressed designs of champlevé are etched into the metal using acid-etching techniques. With metal clay, we can easily add texture and designs using rubber stamps, texture plates, or other simple clay-working tools.

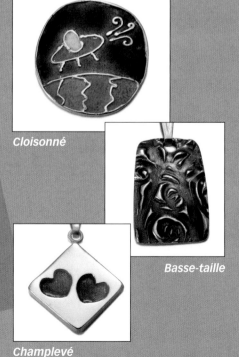

Cloisonné

Basse-taille

Champlevé

Choosing enamels

cleanliness and setting up

Before you begin working with your enamels, take a moment to clear away all your metal clay tools and supplies, and wipe down your work area with a damp cloth. Working in a clean area will avoid introducing contaminants into your enamels and causing unfortunate results. As with metal clay, it's helpful to have all your tools and materials in place before you begin.

enamel types and colors

Now comes the fun part … choosing your enamels! If you want to see the silver through the enamel, choose a transparent color (Thompson 2000 series). For opaque coverage, choose an opaque enamel (Thompson 1000 series).

Choosing specific colors is not as straightforward as it might sound, especially when working on silver. Silver itself is a colorant and can affect the colors you fire onto it. For your first enameling efforts I highly recommend choosing blues or greens, as these fire on silver with no problem.

If you want warm colors, such as reds, pinks, and oranges, you are in for a challenge. These are very tricky colors to fire onto silver. Most often they will turn a yellowish or brownish color, and they may cloud up as well. I am going to suggest two different methods appropriate for those who are relatively new to enameling.

The first is making color change work for you. You won't get red or pink enamel this way, but you can get a very nice orange or yellow. Thompson 2835 Rose Pink fires to a lovely orange on silver. I like to use Thompson 2830 Orange Red Ruby to get a nice warm yellow.

Your second option is to use one of the various leaded enamel colors that are specifically formulated for silver. Ninomiya and Nihon Shippo are Japanese brands of leaded enamel with several colors for silver. Nihon Shippo G704 is a deep, raspberry red and G701C is a nice pink. Please note that not all leaded reds and pinks will stay true on silver; only those specially formulated for silver. I recommend contacting Enamelwork Supply Co. for specific information about leaded enamel colors (see *Resources,* p. 94).

No matter what colors or enamel brand you choose, I strongly recommend testing the colors before you apply them to your metal clay piece. Get a small sheet of 28-gauge fine silver (do not use sterling), and use lightweight metal shears to cut it into small pieces. You can then test your colors on these pieces before firing them on to your metal clay jewelry. This will give you an indication of the true color and firing properties.

Your 80-mesh enamels will have a consistency similar to sugar.

Warm colors on silver are a challenge. Thompson 2835, called Rose Pink, actually produces a very nice orange.

opaques

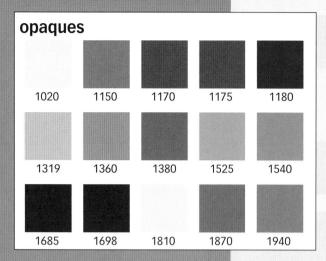

1020	1150	1170	1175	1180
1319	1360	1380	1525	1540
1685	1698	1810	1870	1940

transparents

2110	2115	2120	2130	2140
2170	2190	2220	2222	2230
2305	2310	2320	2325	2335
2340	2350	2410	2420	2430
2435	2520	2530	2610	2625
2650	2660	2680	2715	2755
2760	2835	2910	2915	

The printed colors shown here are only approximations. For best results, test-fire colors on a sample piece.

Enamel color guide

The chart below is from my personal tests and will give you some guidelines for choosing enamel colors. Thompson colors not included on the chart may have shown some difficulty during my tests. The problems could have been as simple as some minor browning around the edges to severe color change. For troublesome opaques, most problems can be avoided by first firing a layer of 2020 Clear for Silver onto the metal. This can help somewhat with transparent enamels too, but it's not quite as effective since the 2020 can give the color a yellowish cast and will not always stop color change. If you want to try problematic colors, test them carefully first. The colors listed below should require no special handling and are good colors for beginners.

THOMPSON STOCK NUMBERS	COLOR
1020	Opaque Titanium White
1150 through **1180**	Opaque Browns
1319, 1360, 1380	Opaque Greens
1525, 1540, 1685, 1698	Opaque Blues
1940	Opaque Steel Gray
1995, 1996, 1997	Opaque Black (not pictured)
2020	Clear for Silver (not pictured)
2110 through **2190**	Transparent Browns
2220, 2222, 2230	Transparent Yellows
2305 through **2350**	Transparent Greens
2410 through **2435**	Transparent Green Blues
2520, 2530	Transparent Blue Greens
2610, 2625, 2650, 2660, 2680	Transparent Blues
2715, 2755, 2760	Transparent Purples
2910, 2915	Transparent Grays

If you are feeling a bit more adventurous, try these:

THOMPSON STOCK NUMBERS	COLOR
1810	Opaque Buttercup Yellow *Wet-pack only. Do not sift. Better over 2020.*
1870	Opaque Orient Red *Fire over 2020. Take care not to over-fire.*
2007 through **2040**	Clears (not pictured) – *All work to varying degrees; may yellow.*
2835	*This color is called Rose Pink, but it usually fires to a lovely transparent orange on metal clay. Use as Orange.*

Preparing enamels

Little, if anything, needs to be done to opaque enamels before you use them. Transparent enamels can be used straight from the jar, just like the opaques; however, the results may be cloudy and muted, giving a translucent, rather than transparent, effect. You can greatly improve the color and clarity of transparent enamel by screening or washing it first. Clarifying the enamel by screening or washing removes the fine particles that can cause cloudiness.

No matter which method you choose, clarify only as much enamel as you are going to use for your current project. Enamel degrades over time, so attempting to process all your enamel at once is not particularly productive. You probably will need to wash it again the next time, so process only as much as you think you will need.

Remember, opaque enamels do not need to be clarified.

screening enamels

Screening is by far the easiest way to clarify your transparent enamels, and it's the method I use most often.

SAFETY NOTE: Always wear at least an N95 or N100 dust mask when screening enamels. This process puts a lot of enamel dust into the air and it's important to adequately protect your lungs.

[1] Take a 4-in. (10cm)-square piece of 200-mesh enamel screen and fold the edges up to form a shallow box. Prepare a clean plastic spoon by using a permanent marker to write the color number or name on the handle.

[2] Place the screen box over a clean piece of paper. Place a small amount of enamel in the box along with a clean coin. The coin will help push the enamel through the screen. Gently shake the box from side to side, sifting out the fine particles.

[3] Once you have removed all the fines, pour what remains in the sifter into the plastic spoon. Set the labeled spoon aside until you are ready to apply the enamel. The fines that have been sifted out may be reserved for future use as counter-enamel or for enamel painting projects; do not mix them back into the rest of your enamel.

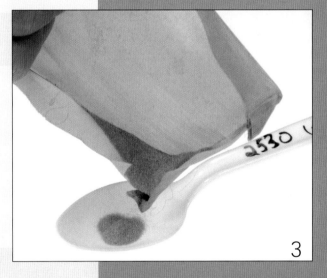

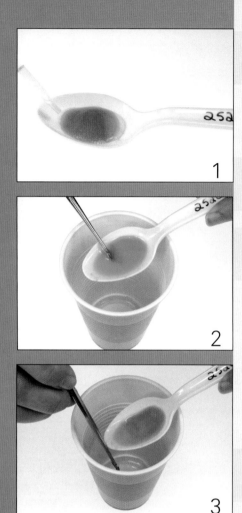

washing enamels

Washing enamels is a more tedious process than screening, but is also an effective way of preparing enamels for use. Many people prefer it, since you don't have to worry about enamel dust in the air. Also, done correctly, it may remove more fines than screening.

[1] Fill a plastic cup with distilled water. Have a second, empty cup on hand. Prepare a clean plastic spoon by using a permanent marker to write the color name or number on the handle. Place a small amount of enamel in the spoon. Use a pipette or eyedropper to add distilled water, filling the spoon until the water generously covers the enamel.

[2] Use a small enamel spoon to agitate the enamel. The enamel, being heavier, will settle down to the bottom of the spoon and the water will become cloudy.

[3] Pour the water into the empty cup (not back into your clean distilled water), holding the enamel spoon against the edge of the plastic spoon to help draw off the water.

Repeat the steps until the water no longer appears cloudy. (You can greatly reduce the number of times this is necessary by screening the enamel before you begin washing it.) Set the enamel in the labeled spoon aside until you are ready to apply it. You will usually wet-pack enamel that you clarify this way.

Enamel application

There are two basic ways of applying enamel to metal: wet-packing or sifting. Wet-packing will give you the greatest amount of control over your results and is the most appropriate for small jewelry projects. Sifting is generally used for larger projects such as bowls and plates; however, it can be useful when covering an entire piece and for applying subtle shading.

preparing the silver

Before applying the enamel to your piece, you need to clean the silver thoroughly. No oils, dust, soaps, or sanding grits should remain, as these can mar your enamels. Use ammonia and a glass brush to clean the piece. Wear rubber or latex gloves to avoid getting glass fibers in your fingers. Rinse and dry the piece.

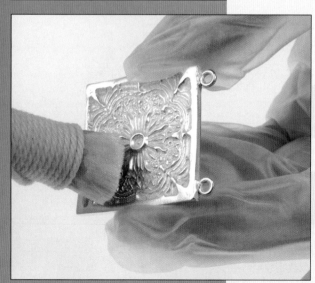

Thoroughly clean the piece with clear ammonia and a glass brush.

tip

Use only clear ammonia. Do not use sudsing or scented ammonia that could contain soaps or detergents.

wet-packing enamels

You'll need a fine paintbrush (liner #10/0 or #1) and a scribe. I also highly recommend a magnifying visor and a good task light for this technique. In general, Klyr-Fire enamel adhesive is not necessary for wet-packing. An exception would be in cases of three-dimensional enameling where you need the enamel to stick to an area that's not flat. In that case, just a drop or two of Klyr-Fire added to the enamel and water will be sufficient.

[1] Prepare your silver and enamels as described previously. Whether you clarify your enamels or not, each color you are going to use should be in a clean plastic spoon marked with the color name or number.

[2] Use a plastic pipette or eyedropper to add enough distilled water to cover the enamel. Rather than mixing like a paint or paste, the enamel grains will settle in the water like sand. You need enough water to allow the enamel movement and flow. You should be able to move a brush through it easily.

[3] Pick up a small amount of enamel with the brush and lay it onto the piece. Use the scribe to push the enamel off the brush and onto the silver. You also can use the point of the scribe to move the particles of enamel around, positioning them where you like. If the enamel does move easily onto the silver, it may be too dry. Add more distilled water to the enamel.

[4] Continue adding enamel until you have covered all areas that you want enameled. You can apply more than one color at a time. It is not necessary to fire each color separately. Colors may also be blended where they come together to create shading effects. Keep the layer of enamel thin. It's tempting to want to pile on the enamel to reduce the number of firings necessary, but this can result in air bubbles or pits in your finished piece.

[5] Once all the enamel is in place, pick up the piece and tap the edge with the handle of a fairly hefty tool, like the scribe handle (a paintbrush handle is too light). Tapping the piece settles the enamel and brings the water to the surface. If the enamel is too dry and does not settle when tapped, use the pipette to carefully add a drop of water to the enamel and tap it again.

[6] Hold a piece of paper towel to the edge of the enamel to draw off the excess moisture.

(continued on p. 38)

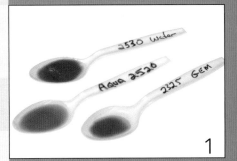

1

2

3

4

5

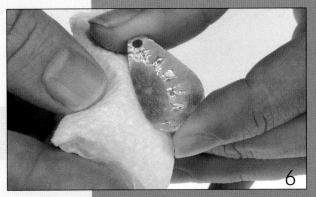

6

Enameling on Metal Clay

37

Getting Started

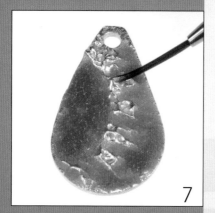

7

wet-packing enamels (continued)

[7] Use your magnifying visor to carefully examine the front and back of the piece for stray enamel. Use a clean brush to sweep it away, or to push it back into the enameled areas. The nonenameled areas should be as free of enamel as possible before firing.

[8] Place the piece on a trivet or mica sheet on a firing rack, and place it on top of the kiln to dry. The enamel must be dry before firing, or you may end up with bubbles or pits. Drying takes only a few minutes. The enamel will have a light, granular look when dry.

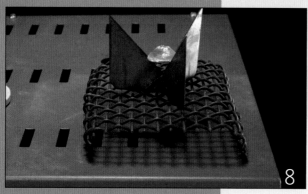

8

sifting enamels

Prepare your silver and enamel as described previously. If you wish to clarify the transparent enamel, use the screening method only.

You will need a small sifter, clean paper, a small enamel spoon, and Klyr-Fire enamel adhesive. Prepare your Klyr-Fire by diluting it 1:1 with distilled water in a sprayer.

Lightly mist your piece with Klyr-Fire. Do not spray directly on the piece, but rather spray above it and let the mist settle onto the silver. Spray off to one side rather than over your clean paper and enamels.

[1] Place a small amount of enamel in the sifter. Hold the sifter over the piece and run your fingernail over the twisted handle of the sifter. This will vibrate the tool and cause the enamel to sift out. Move the sifter around, covering the piece with a layer of enamel. You can use more than one color for subtle shading effects if desired.

[2] Pick the piece up by the edges and look underneath to check for stray enamel, and clean off any stray grains. Place the piece in a clean trivet on a firing rack. Allow the enamel adhesive to dry for a few minutes before firing.

NOTE: Any sifted project can be wet-packed as an alternative.

1

2

Counter-enameling

Counter-enameling is just a fancy way of saying a piece will have enamel on both the front and the back. Enamels can stress the metal, causing it to warp slightly, resulting in cracks or chips. By putting enamel on the back of the piece, the stress is equalized and no cracking should occur.

It's not always necessary to counter-enamel. If the metal is thick enough, and/or the enamel is very thin, or if only a small portion of the piece is being enameled, counter-enamel may not be necessary. A domed shape is less prone to warping and may not need counter-enameling. But counter-enameling is not difficult, and it will never hurt your piece, so I do recommend it.

Ideally, enamel should be applied to both the front and back of the piece at the same time; however, this can be tricky for beginners. If you attempt it, you will need to include Klyr-Fire enamel adhesive in your counter-enamel to prevent it from dropping off. To start with, I recommend enameling in two steps, firing the counter-enamel before enameling the front.

Choose a color for the back that is the same or lighter than the color you are applying to the front of the piece. That way if any stray enamel fires onto the front during the counter-enameling, it will not be a problem. This is a good use for the fines that were sifted out during the enamel prep stage.

Counter-enamel can be either sifted on or wet-packed. In either case, start with a thoroughly clean piece (see *Preparing the silver,* p. 36). These instructions are for sifted application.

[1] Brush the back with full-strength Klyr-Fire rather than just misting the piece. If the Klyr-Fire beads up instead of covering the area, your piece is not yet clean enough – you need to really scrub it. Apply a generous amount of Klyr-Fire. It can even pool a bit in the middle of the piece. This will allow a thicker application of enamel.

[2] Start sifting onto the outer edges of the piece. Allow the enamel around the edges to soak up some of the Klyr-Fire from the middle before sifting over the whole piece. Don't let the enamel thin out at the edges.

[3] Try for a nice, even application across the entire back of the piece.

(To apply the counter-enamel by wet-packing rather than sifting, follow the instructions for wet-packing on p. 37, adding several drops of Klyr-Fire along with the water in step 2.)

[4] A small spatula is helpful for picking up the piece and moving it to a trivet without disturbing the enamel. Place the piece on a trivet that supports only the edges so the enameled surfaces do not touch anything during firing. Whether you sifted the enamel or wet-packed it, give it a few minutes on top of the kiln to dry. When you fire it, fuse only to the orange-peel stage. The counter-enamel will continue to smooth out as you fire the enamels onto the front of the piece.

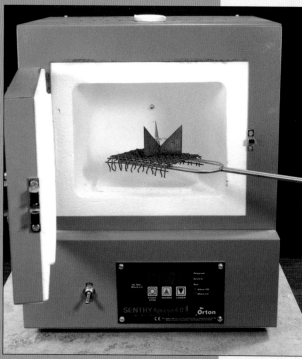

Use a firing fork and heat-resistant gloves to move the firing rack in and out of the hot kiln.

Firing enamels

using a programmable kiln

Unlike metal clay, enamels cannot be placed in a cold kiln and brought up to temperature. The kiln must be preheated to the desired temperature before firing the enamels. Needless to say, taking items in and out of a hot kiln requires some care. You will need a firing rack, a firing fork, and heat-resistant gloves, as well as a selection of trivets or mica sheets. A pair of long bentnose tweezers are also handy for moving hot pieces. You should have a pair of green IR filter safety glasses to protect your eyes when looking into the hot kiln.

Enamels fuse between 1400°F (760°C) and 1500°F (815°C). Kilns will lose heat when you open the door, especially the encased element kilns like the Paragon SC series. You have a limited amount of time to make up the loss. I usually set mine between 1450°F (785°C) and 1500°F (815°C). Traditional brick kilns hold the heat better and can be set between 1425°F (775°C) and 1475°F (800°C).

Enameling is a function of time and temperature. If you set your kiln at the lower end of the fusing range, you will have longer firing times. If you set your kiln at the higher end, you will have shorter firing times. It's better for beginners to work lower and slower as you'll be less likely to over-fire your enamels. You can always put the piece back in if it's not done, but you can't undo over-firing, so be patient and take your time.

The firing itself is not difficult or complicated. Use the firing fork and heat-resistant gloves to move the firing rack, with the piece on it, into the hot kiln and close the door. Begin timing the firing for 2 minutes and then open the door and check the piece. Be sure to wear your filtered safety glasses when looking into the kiln. If the enamel is fused, you can use the firing fork to take it out. Otherwise close the door and continue timing for another minute or two. Some kiln models have a window or peephole in the door, which allows you to check the stage of the firing without opening the door.

If you are applying multiple layers of enamel, you can fire the first layers to just the orange-peel stage, and then apply the next coat over that. Only the final coat needs to be taken to the smooth and glossy stage. This will help avoid over-firing the enamels over the course of multiple firings. Allow each firing to cool before applying the next layer.

preparing a programmable kiln

If you are using an SC model kiln, you'll find the door latch can be very tight. This is fine for metal clay, but can present a problem when working with enamels. If the unit is jarred too much when the door is closed, the enamel can be displaced. Fortunately, this is easy to fix. The door latch has two spring-loaded bearings that hold it secure when closed. Each bearing is held in place by a set screw that can be loosened. I chose to completely remove the bottom bearing from my latch. The top bearing still holds the door secure, but not so tight that I can't easily open and close the door without jarring my enamels.

Programming the Orton Sentry Xpress 4.0 Controller is slightly different for enameling than it is for metal clay. Instead of shutting off after a short hold time, you want the kiln to remain at temperature until you manually shut it off.

To allow the kiln door to open and close smoothly, you can loosen the set screws in the door latch's two spring-loaded bearings.

controller settings for enameling

[1] Press the **Start/Stop** button until the display reads **Pr0** or **SPd** followed by a number.

[2] Press the **HIGHER** button until you reach **Pr01**. If you scroll past your target, do not use the **LOWER** button. Just continue using the **HIGHER** button until **Pr01** comes around again.

[3] Press the **Start/Stop** button again to move to the next programming segment.

[4] The display will now read **rA 1**, alternating with the desired ramp speed. Press the **HIGHER** button until the display reads **FULL**.

[5] Press the **Start/Stop** button.

[6] The display will read **°F 1**, alternating with the programmed temperature. Press the **HIGHER** or **LOWER** buttons until the display reaches the desired firing temperature. For enameling this will be between 1450°F (785°C) and 1500°F (815°C).

[7] Press the **Start/Stop** button.

[8] The display will read **HLd1**, alternating with the set hold time. Press the **HIGHER** or **LOWER** buttons until the display reaches **99.59**.

[9] Press the **Start/Stop** button.

[10] The display will read **rA 2**. Press the **HIGHER** or **LOWER** buttons until the display reaches **0000**.

[11] Press the **Start/Stop** button two more times. The first time, **Strt** will display. The second time, **-ON-** will display.

The kiln will commence heating to the set temperature at this point and will hold until you manually shut off the kiln. **Pr01** is now set for enameling. The next time you can just use the **LOWER** button after reaching **Pr01** to review the program and launch the kiln for enameling.

Sheet mica protects a piece from the buildup on the firing rack.

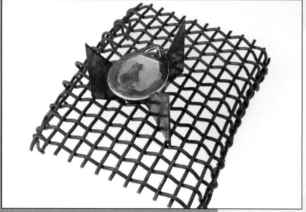

Trivets are especially handy for holding counter-enameled pieces.

Use the small spatula that comes with the UltraLite to move pieces in and out.

using sheet mica

Sheet mica protects your work during firing. Firing racks tend to become encrusted with carbon and old enamel over time. Rather than set the piece directly on the rack, place it on a sheet of mica on the rack. Use mica only when you are not applying counter-enamel. Sheet mica is thin, clear, and stiff when you first get it. Cut it with scissors to create smaller pieces. After repeated firings it will start to delaminate, becoming opaque and puffing up a bit. It will also lose some of its rigidity. Replace mica that is too soft to hold your work or is coming apart.

using trivets

Trivets hold a piece by the edges, allowing you to enamel both sides without the enamel sticking to your firing rack. Place the trivet on the firing rack to move it in and out of the kiln. It's important to always fire on a clean trivet. Over time enamel may collect on your trivet, sticking to your piece or causing unwanted marks. You can remove the enamel by heating the trivet in the kiln and then dropping it into a bucket of water. The thermal shock will break off most of the enamel. What remains can be sanded off.

safety note

Hot trivets look just like cold trivets! Never pick up a trivet with your fingers. Always use tweezers or tongs. Don't ask me how I know. Ouch!

firing enamel in an UltraLite

Firing in an UltraLite kiln is not unlike firing in a regular kiln. Preheat the UltraLite for 20 to 30 minutes before you begin. Setting one of the ceramic inserts on top of the lid will help hold in the heat. The piece to be enameled may be set on a small piece of sheet mica or on a low-profile trivet. Use the small spatula or a pair of long bentnose tweezers to move the piece in and out of the UltraLite. Because the unit is not as well insulated as a regular kiln, it may take slightly longer to fuse the enamel.

firing enamel on a gas stovetop

Stovetop firing won't work for all techniques, but it can be quick, easy, and fun. If your project is small and flat or only very slightly domed, and you are only applying one or two thin layers of enamel, it can work quite well. Stovetop firing does not allow you to counter-enamel.

[1] Place a stainless-steel wire mesh screen on your gas burner and turn the flame on high. Fairly quickly, red hot spots will appear. Make note of where these are and turn off the burner.

[2] Use a pair of long bentnose tweezers to gently place your piece on one of the hot spots and turn the burner back on high. If you've missed the spot, use the tweezers to adjust the position of the screen, not the piece. Trying to move the piece may upset the enamel. Keep an eye on the enamel, and when it reaches the smooth and glossy stage, turn off the burner. You can use the tweezers to move the piece to a kiln shelf or firing rack to cool.

SAFETY NOTE: Never fire leaded enamels on a stovetop or with a torch because harmful vapors may be released.

firing enamel with a butane torch

Torch-firing enamels on metal clay can be somewhat tricky. Like stovetop firing, this is not a method that you can use if you need to counter-enamel, and it is only good for one or two thin coats of enamel. Also, like the gas stove, the heat must come from below the piece. Attempting to top-fire it can cause the enamel to ball up, pull away from the edges, and possibly discolor.

To torch-fire, stand two firing bricks on end and place a large firing rack across them to create a firing table. This should allow you to get your torch underneath. What makes this method really tricky is the danger of melting your piece. I recommend using a butane torch. Any other type of torch may get too hot for the silver.

Set your piece on the rack and turn on your torch. Move the torch flame in a circular pattern around the underside of the piece. You need to keep your eye on two things: the fusing of the enamel and the color of the silver. Do not allow the silver to get any brighter than a pale salmon-pink color. If it starts to turn orange or get brighter, back off. Once the enamel reaches the smooth and glossy stage, turn off the torch and allow the piece to cool.

Small pieces can be fired from below with a butane torch.

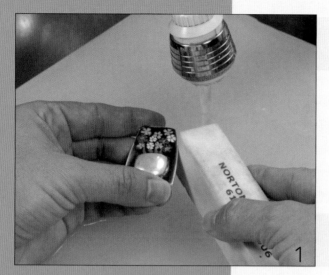

Enamel finishing

When you are done with your piece, any exposed silver may have a dull or whitish cast again. You also may have fired a few grains of enamel onto areas you wanted kept clear. Bringing the silver areas back to a high shine will give your piece a finished, professional look.

IMPORTANT NOTE: All enamel grinding and sanding should be done wet. If you work dry, you may chip or crack your enamel. I usually work at my kitchen sink with a rubber block. I let the tap run very lightly onto the block, keeping my piece wet as I work.

[1] Grind off any stray bits of enamel with an alundum stone. This will leave scratches that will have to be sanded out, so decide beforehand if you want to live with the excess enamel or if you are prepared for more sanding.

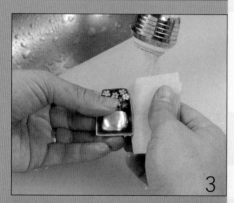

[2] If you used the alundum stone or didn't finish the silver before enameling, use 400-, 600-, and 1200-grit sandpapers to sand out the scratches. Take care when sanding to focus on the silver and avoid the enamel as much as possible. You don't want to scratch it. See *Mirror finishing* on p. 30 for specific sanding instructions.

[3] If you did not need to use the alundum stone, and your piece was well-finished before enameling, it won't take much to take the silver back up to a high shine at this point. Usually just the blue, pink, and mint Tri-M-Ite polish papers are all you will need. Again, focus on the silver and avoid the enamel.

[4] As a final step, apply a little metal polish to the silver areas with your finger and use a soft flannel cloth to buff it to a high shine. You can also use a Sunshine polish cloth without applying metal polish.

Removing enamel

When enamel bonds with metal, it really bonds! This is a big reason I suggest testing your enamels before applying them to your piece.

When the results are a surprise, sometimes you can learn to love what you've got, no matter how unexpected. There was a time when most enamelists would have told you to do just that.

Here is a little-known way to remove that tenacious enamel so you can save the precious silver piece and start again. It uses simple household ingredients: ordinary table salt, cream of tartar, and a small dish of water. (Cream of tartar can be found in the baking section of your local grocery store.) You will heat your UltraLite or programmable kiln to enamel-fusing temperature (between 1400°F/760°C and 1500°F/815°C). Have a cup of very cold water waiting for the rinse.

You cannot selectively remove enamel using this technique. You will remove it all and start over. Because the paste smokes as it burns, be sure to do this with good ventilation.

[1] Mix equal parts salt and cream of tartar. Add just enough water to make it into a creamy paste.

[2] Apply the paste to the enameled sections of your piece.

[3] Place the piece on a sheet of mica before putting it in your UltraLite or kiln. Heat the piece to enamel-fusing temperature. The paste will bubble and boil as the water content steams off.

[4] As the paste continues to heat, it will begin to turn brown and then black.

[5] Continue firing. It needs to remain at this black stage for a while. The trick to making this technique work is cooking it long enough. Fire it for at least 2 to 4 minutes. It will smoke and smell fairly unpleasant while the paste is burning.

Use a pair of tweezers to move the piece directly from the heat source (wear gloves if you are using a kiln), and drop it into a cup of very cold water.

[6] The black crust may break off in the water, or it may remain stuck to the piece. Use the tip of the tweezers to break away the crust that is stuck.

[7] Use a stiff steel-wire brush and water to scrub away the remainder of the black residue.

Depending on how much enamel was on the piece to begin with, you may have to repeat this process a couple of times to remove all the enamel.

This technique was developed and taught by master engraver Gilberto Mazzotti of São Paulo, Brazil. My sincere thanks to Priscilla Vassao for sharing it with me.

before

after

1

2

3

4

5

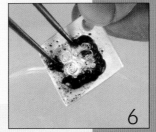

6

7

Projects

At last – the fun part of the book! The eight projects presented
in this section will introduce you to a wide range of metal clay
and enameling techniques. Different projects use different
techniques: stamping, stacking, and syringing metal clay; sifting
and wet-packing enamels – all with various firing options.
Whichever methods you choose to explore, I know you're going
to love your finished pieces, and you'll be delighted when you
find out how easy it really is. So let's get started.

quick & easy earrings

Introduction to basic techniques

firing methods
Metal clay: programmable kiln, butane torch, UltraLite, or gas stovetop
Enamel: programmable kiln, UltraLite, or gas stovetop

tools & supplies

Metal clay
- Metal clay tools (p. 11-13)
- Metal clay firing tools and equipment (p. 16-18)
- 10g metal clay
- Clay shape cutter (optional)
- Texture stamp
- Rubber stamp

Enameling
- Enameling tools (p. 14-15)
- Enamel firing tools and equipment (p. 16-18)
- *Thompson lead-free 80-mesh enamels:*
  2230 Transparent Lime Yellow
  2115 Transparent Mars Brown
  2190 Transparent Chestnut Brow[n]
  1685 Opaque Cobalt Blue

Finishing
- Ear wires
- Silver jump rings
- Chainnose pliers
- Flatnose pliers

These fun earrings are, without a doubt, the easiest project in this book and the best ones to start with if you have never enameled or worked with metal clay before. There is no counter-enameling involved, and you can fire them using a gas stovetop or an UltraLite kiln.

I demonstrate two ways to create the earrings. For the first pair, we'll apply an overall texture, then sift the enamels. For the second pair, I show stamping an image and wet-packing the enamels. Both methods are quick and easy, and either will give you beautiful results. I suggest trying both as this will give you a good introduction to the basic techniques in this book.

making the textured earrings

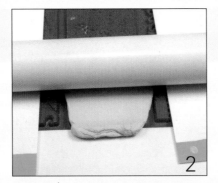

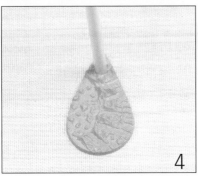

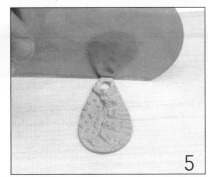

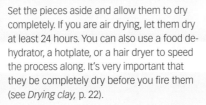

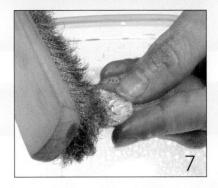

Prepare your work space and tools. Apply Badger Balm or olive oil to your hands, roller, and nonstick work surface (see *Preparing your work space,* p. 20). Lightly coat the texture stamp with olive oil as well. Tap the flat end of a stencil brush on a sponge saturated with olive oil, and then tap the brush on the texture **[1]**. This forces the olive oil down into the detail, but maintains a very light, thin coat. Oil should not pool in your texture stamp.

Place a pair of blue slats a few inches apart on your texture stamp. Place the clay on the stamp, between the slats, and use the roller to roll it out, keeping the ends on the slats **[2]** (see *Rolling clay,* p. 22). Remove the clay and turn it textured side up on the work surface.

Cut two matching shapes for your earrings. You can use small cookie cutters, a craft knife, or any other cutting tool **[3]**.

Use a small straw to make a hole in each piece, so the clay pieces can hang from jump rings **[4]**. If you dip the end of the straw in Badger Balm before cutting your hole, you'll be able to blow out the small bit of clay stuck in the straw fairly easily when you're done.

If your piece comes to a point, like the one in this example, cut the point off above the hole so the earring can move freely after it's attached to a jump ring **[5]**.

Set the pieces aside and allow them to dry completely. If you are air drying, let them dry at least 24 hours. You can also use a food dehydrator, a hotplate, or a hair dryer to speed the process along. It's very important that they be completely dry before you fire them (see *Drying clay,* p. 22).

Once the pieces are dry, use sandpaper or sponge-backed sanding pads to smooth any rough edges **[6]** (see *Greenware finishing,* p. 23). Use a round file to clean up the hole for the jump ring.

The earrings are now ready to be fired. This can be done using any of the available firing methods. This project lends itself to stovetop or UltraLite firing (see *Firing metal clay,* p. 26).

After the earring pieces have been fired and cooled, they need to be burnished. Begin by brushing them vigorously with a brass-wire brush, soap, and water **[7]**. Final burnishing can be done by hand with a burnisher, or in a rotary tumbler with stainless steel shot (see *Postfire finishing,* p. 29). Your earrings are now ready for enameling.

enameling the earrings

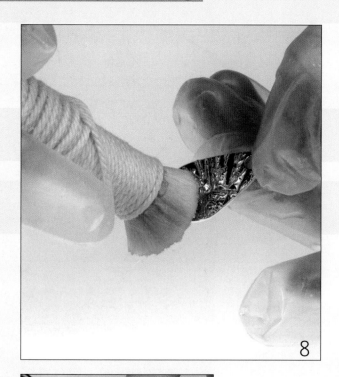

8

9

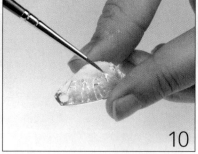

10

Choose your colors and prepare your enamels (see *Preparing enamels,* p. 35). For this first project, I used Lime Yellow, Mars Brown, and Chestnut Brown; all are very easy colors to work with.

Clean each earring with a glass brush dipped in clear ammonia to remove any dirt, oils, or soap left from the burnishing **[8]**. Rinse with clean water and dry. Wear latex or rubber gloves to protect your fingers from the glass fibers.

Lightly mist the piece with Klyr-Fire enamel adhesive. Klyr-Fire should be diluted 1:1 with water. Do not spray directly onto the piece; spray above it and let the mist settle down onto it. Place the piece on a clean sheet of paper.

Pour a little dry enamel into a ½-in. (13mm) sifter. Hold the sifter over the piece and run your fingernail along the twisted handle, vibrating the tool and gently sifting out the

enamel **[9]**. Additional colors may be sifted on to create shading or color variation.

Use a small paintbrush to gently clear the enamel from the high points of the piece **[10]**. Use your finger to clear any stray enamel from the edges and back of the piece. Lightly mist the piece with Klyr-Fire again. This will prevent the enamel from dislodging when you move it to the firing screen.

three stages of enamel firing

granular

orange peel

glossy and smooth

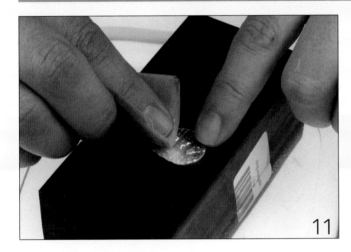

11

tip

Although this project lends itself to stovetop firing, feel free to use your kiln for either firing step – the metal clay firing or the enamel firing.

Place the piece on the firing screen for stovetop firing, or on a small piece of mica for UltraLite firing (see *Firing enamels,* p. 40).

Watch the enamel as it fuses. It will first appear granular, then it will proceed to an orange-peel stage, and finally it will smooth out to a glossy surface (see *Three stages of enamel firing,* above).

When it reaches the glossy and smooth state, remove it from the heat source and let the piece cool. You can repeat the enameling steps if you would like to fill in areas that were missed, or to provide deeper color or shading; however, I do not recommend more than two layers. If the enamel gets too thick, it could crack.

Use Tri-M-Ite polishing paper to shine up the high points, sides, and backs of the earring pieces, but take care not to sand the enamel. All silver sanding or polishing should be done wet after the enamels have been applied **[11]**.

Give the pieces a final buff with a polishing cloth to bring the silver to a high shine (see *Enamel finishing,* page 44).

Continue with *Assembling the earrings* on p. 53 to finish the textured earrings.

making the stamped earrings

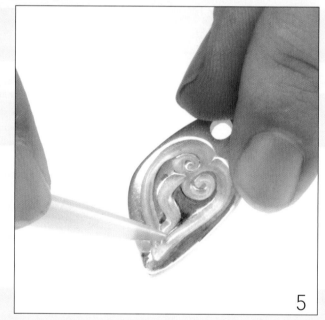

Begin as you did for the textured earrings by preparing your work space and tools, and by applying a thin coat of olive oil to your rubber stamp **[1]**.

Roll the clay to an even thickness using the red slats. Carefully stamp the image into the clay **[2]**. Use a small straw to create a hole for the jump ring **[3]**. Use a craft knife to cut around the image and hole, creating the shape for your earring **[4]**.

Set it aside to dry and make a second, matching piece. Once the earrings are dry, sand and smooth away any rough edges as in step 6 of the textured earrings instructions.

Fire, brush, and burnish them. These earrings are easy to hand burnish using an agate burnisher **[5]**.

applying the enamels

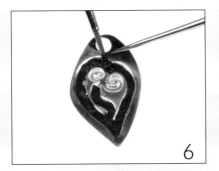

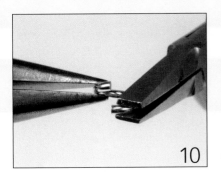

Prepare the silver as you did before, cleaning it with ammonia and a glass brush. For this pair, you will wet-pack the enamel rather than sift it. I chose Cobalt Blue for these. Because cobalt is an opaque color, it is not necessary to prescreen it.

Prepare your enamel for wet-packing. Begin laying the enamel into the pattern using a fine paintbrush and a scribe **[6]** (see *Wet-packing enamels,* p. 37). Tap the edge of the piece to

settle the enamel **[7]**. Use a piece of paper towel to wick away excess moisture **[8]**.

Use a clean brush to remove any enamel that has strayed out of the design **[9]**. You can either brush it away or push it back into the design. Use a magnifying visor and a good task light to be sure you catch all the grains.

Let the enamel dry and then fire as you did for the sifted-enamel earrings.

assembling the earrings

Always open jump rings as shown. Use two pairs of pliers to grasp the ring ends. Move one pair toward you and the other away **[10]**.

Slide the earring and ear wire onto the jump ring **[11]**. To add interest and movement, you can add a silver bead or beaded dangles.

Close the jump ring by reversing the movement you used in step 10, and you're done **[12]**. Congratulations!

check stray grains before firing

It's always easier to remove stray enamel before it's fired rather than to try to grind off unwanted enamel later. A magnifying visor and a good task light will help ensure you do not miss any grains.

54

kaleidoscope fantasy

firing methods
Metal clay: programmable kiln or UltraLite
Enamel: programmable kiln or UltraLite

Reversible pendant with warm-color, leaded enamels

Firing warm colors – reds, oranges, yellows, pinks, and some purples – on silver can be challenging. Silver is a colorant and will normally turn these colors to yellow or brown. There are a number of ways to deal with this, but one of the easiest is to use leaded enamels that are specifically formulated to fire on silver. Take a few extra precautions when using leaded enamels (see p. 56). These steps aren't too difficult and the rewards are worth the effort.

A rubber stamp creates the focal pattern of this pendant. Look for a design that can be enhanced and highlighted with color. I used a floral square from a multiple-texture stamp. It was ideal for two reasons: It had a nice pattern to be colored and a raised border that frames and finishes the pendant.

tools & supplies

Metal clay
- Metal clay tools (p. 11-13)
- Metal clay firing tools and equipment (p. 16-18)
- 35g metal clay
- Metal clay paste
- Metal clay syringe
- Rubber texture stamp
- 4 large fine-silver flat-eye screws
- Drinking straw

Enameling
- Enameling tools (p. 14-15)
- Enamel firing tools and equipment (p. 16-18)
- *Japanese leaded 80-mesh enamels (transparent):*
  Nihon Shippo **G704** Red
  Ninomiya **N26** Med. Yellow
  Ninomiya **N23** Dark Gold
  Ninomiya **L82** Med. Blue Purple

Finishing
- Silk cords or silver chain

making the pendant and bail

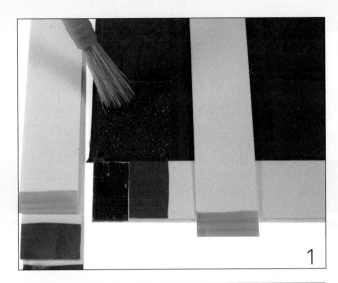

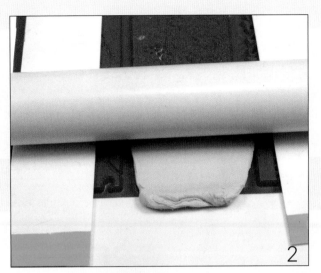

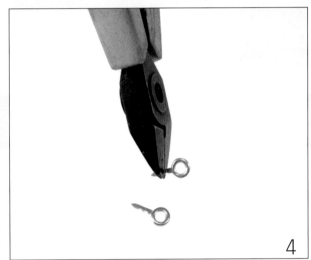

Prepare tools and work space for working with metal clay (see *Preparing your work space,* p. 20). Prepare your stamp by using a stencil brush to apply a very thin coat of olive oil **[1]**. The oil should not pool in the pattern.

Before rolling onto the stamp, roll the clay to an even thickness using a stack of red and yellow slats. Try to get the clay to match the size and shape of the stamp. Rolling a thick slab this way will make it easier to get the image into the clay without any stretching or distortion. Rolling clay onto a corner stamp can be a challenge, but the graduated slats make it a lot easier. (For this stamp, I made one stack of purple and red next to the stamp and another across the top of the stamp, creating a frame that was the same height as my stamp. Next I added the blue slats, one on the stack and one on the stamp.) Roll the clay onto the stamp **[2]**.

Peel the clay off the stamp, place it on a non-stick work surface, and trim the edges. Insert the fine-silver flat-eye screws into the top of the piece and set it aside **[3]**.

Before starting the bail, trim about half the stem from two fine-silver flat-eye screws **[4]**. (If left long, they will stick up into the interior space of the bail and interfere with the stringing cord or chain.)

tip

If you have a large stamp and want to use just part of it, that's fine! You can leave it without a raised border or add one using syringe clay. It will not affect the enamel application either way. The border is purely aesthetic, not functional.

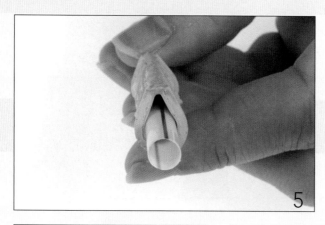

5

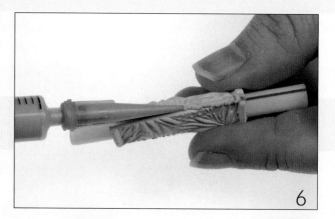

6

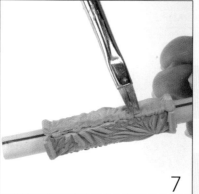

7

8

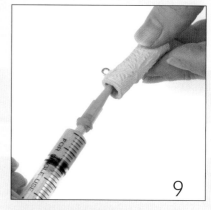

9

10

To create the bail, repeat the steps you used to roll out the pendant. You can use the same stamp or a different image. I chose a different square on the same texture mat for my project. When you trim the clay, you can leave a border on two edges, giving it the same aesthetic as the pendant. You will need to trim off the excess from the other two edges to make it the right length for wrapping around the straw.

Wrap the piece around the straw. Form a teardrop-shape bail **[5]**. This will allow larger cords or chains to fit. Seal the seam with

syringe **[6]** and smooth it into place with a damp brush **[7]**.

When inserting the flat-eye screws into the seam, be sure to line the bail up with the pendant so the screws will be aligned **[8]**. It's important that you make both the pendant and bail at the same time because metal clay shrinks not only when it's fired, but also as it dries. If you let the pendant dry completely before making the bail, the flat eye screws will not line up correctly. Dry both pieces completely (see *Drying clay,* p. 22).

Remove the straw and use syringe and a damp brush to reinforce both the inside and outside of the seam of the bail **[9]**. Also reinforce all four flat-eye screws **[10]**. Let the reinforcements dry.

Sand and smooth the edges, and do any other greenware finishing needed for both the pendant and the bail (see *Greenware finishing,* p. 23). Fire both pieces using the firing method of your choice. Brush and burnish (see *Postfire finishing,* p. 29).

safety note

When working with leaded enamel, take a few extra safety precautions. Firing leaded enamel can release potentially harmful vapors. You should not fire leaded enamels with a torch or on the stovetop. Also, take care not to over-fire the enamels. You should vent your kiln during firing. This means removing the vent plug that fits in the top of most kilns. You should have an active ventilation system near your kiln as well. This can be an exhaust hood or simply a box fan in a window.

enameling the pendant

11

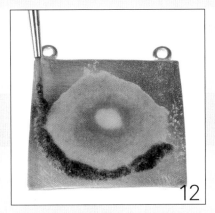

12

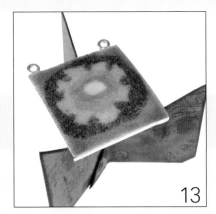

13

14

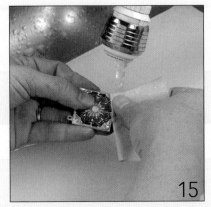

15

16

This flat, square piece offers the opportunity to make an attractive, reversible pendant by enameling the back. Counter-enameling doesn't have to be boring. Have some fun with it!

Clean the back and front of the pendant with ammonia and a glass brush **[11]**. Wear latex or rubber gloves to protect your fingers from the glass fibers. Preheat your kiln to 1425°F-1475°F (775°C-800°C). This is slightly lower than I usually recommend, but it's important not to over-fire leaded enamels, especially reds and yellows. Prepare your enamels for wet-packing and apply them while the kiln is heating up (see *Preparing enamels,* p. 35).

Start with the counter-enamel on the back of the piece (see *Counter-enameling*, p. 39). Working from the center out, lay in your enamel colors **[12]**. You can create blended areas by mixing a small amount of two of your colors in a spoon. Keep in mind enamel does not mix like paint. The enamel grains stay discrete, so you end up with a polka-dot effect you can see if you look at it closely. But from a distance, you get a visual blending of the colors. Apply enamel all the way to the edges of the piece (see *Wet-packing enamels,* p. 37).

Tap the edge of the piece with a heavy tool or tool handle to settle the enamel and bring the water to the surface. Touch a paper towel to the edge of the piece to draw off the excess water. Check the front and edges of the piece to make sure they are free of stray enamel.

Place the piece on a clean trivet **[13]** and set it on a firing rack on top of your kiln to dry. Once the enamel is dry, fire for 2 minutes and then check it (see *Firing enamels,* p. 40). If it's ready, remove it from the kiln; otherwise, fire for another minute and check it again. Fire the counter-enamel only to the orange-peel stage. It will smooth out when the front is fired.

Once the piece has cooled, turn it over and repeat the enamel application steps on the front of the piece, again working from the middle out and blending the colors where they come together, if desired **[14]**. As before, tap to settle the enamel and draw off excess water with a paper towel. Examine the piece carefully with your magnifying visor to look for stray enamel. Use a clean brush to clear any enamel from areas you want to remain silver.

Fire the enamel, taking it all the way to the glossy and smooth stage this time. Keep an eye on it and be careful not to over-fire. Once the piece has cooled, use wet/dry

sandpaper and Tri-M-Ite polishing paper to shine up the non-enameled areas, taking care not to scratch the enamel **[15]**. Remember to work wet when sanding. Give the exposed silver a final buff with a tiny bit of metal polish and a soft flannel polishing cloth (see *Enamel finishing,* p. 44).

Before assembling the pendant, make sure the bail is polished to the same high shine as the pendant. Use jump rings to attach the bail to the pendant **[16]**. String the pendant on colorful silk cord or a silver chain.

golden days of summer

Sifted pendant with gold-foil accents

firing methods
Metal clay: programmable kiln, butane torch, or UltraLite
Enamel: programmable kiln or UltraLite

Adding pure-gold accents will bring a new level of elegance to your enameled jewelry. No one will ever guess how easy it is!

You'll need a small piece of genuine gold foil for this beautiful pendant. What's the difference between *foil* and *leaf*? Gold leaf is less expensive, tissue thin, and thus very difficult to work with. It tends to disintegrate if you even look at it too hard. Gold foil has more body and is easier to apply. Foil is available in both lightweight and heavyweight versions. The lighter-weight foil is more economical and is ideal for this project.

tools & supplies

Metal clay
- Metal clay tools (p. 11-13)
- Metal clay firing tools and equipment (p. 16-18)
- 10g metal clay
- Clay shape cutter (optional)
- Metal clay syringe
- Light bulb
- Floral foam
- Polymer clay (scrap)

Enameling
- Enameling tools (p. 14-15)
- Enamel firing tools and equipment (p. 16-18)
- 23K-24K lightweight gold foil
- Paper-craft punch or nail scissors
- Tweezers
- *Thompson lead-free 80-mesh enamels (transparent):*
  2310 Peppermint Green
  2325 Gem Green
  2350 Grass Green
  2020 Clear for Silver

Finishing
- 52-in. (1.3m) silk cord

creating the pendant

1

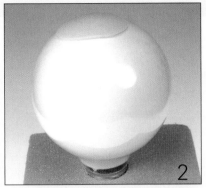

2

tip

Use different sizes of light bulbs for a variety of dome shapes. Plastic Easter eggs are also great for forming domes!

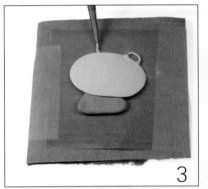

3

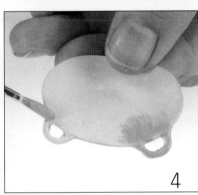

4

5

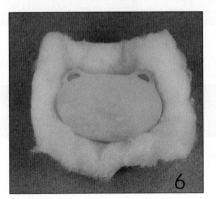

6

tip

Do NOT use the fiber blanket to support projects in an UltraLite. The blanket will insulate the piece too much, and the piece will not get fully fired. You can still fire most domed projects in the Ultra-Lite without the blanket. Place the concave side up to best maintain the domed shape.

Prepare your tools and work area (see *Preparing your work space,* p. 20). Carefully press the base of the light bulb into the floral foam to create a stand.

This piece is domed, making it stronger than a flat piece, so you can roll it out a bit thinner than usual. Try using your blue slats (see *Rolling clay,* p. 22). Cut the pendant shape using a craft knife, cutter/scraper, or a cookie cutter [1].

Place the piece on the light bulb and gently form it to the domed shape [2]. Let the clay dry on the bulb. Remove the dry piece from the light bulb and smooth the greenware (see *Greenware finishing,* p. 23).

Tape a piece of your nonstick work surface to a piece of cardboard to create a stable, flat area that you can easily move without disturbing the syringe work to come. When you set the pendant on the work surface, the top should rest on the surface (this is where you will add the bails). If it doesn't, prop up the bottom with a bit of polymer clay. This should make the top flush with the work surface.

Use a syringe with a large tip to create two bails attached to both sides of the pendant top [3]. Let dry. Reinforce the front and back with more syringe and paste, paying special attention to the area where the bails connect with the pendant [4]. Let dry again and then smooth out this area. You can use a variety of greenware tools including sanding swabs and needle files. I find a damp sponge-tip

applicator is great for this [5]. Use a light touch, as these delicate bails can break off easily at this stage.

When the greenware finishing is done and the piece is completely dry, nest it on a piece of fiber blanket to maintain its curve and fire it [6]. Brush and burnish (see *Postfire finishing,* p. 29).

7

8

9

10

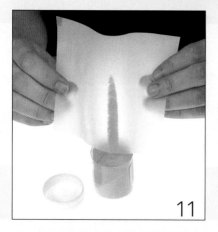

11

Because the domed shape of this piece gives it strength and stability, counter-enameling may not be necessary. If you limit the enamel on the front to just one or two layers, it probably will be fine without it. On the other hand, counter-enameling won't harm your piece and will add to its overall durability. If you decide to skip the counter-enameling steps, this project could be fired on a gas stovetop.

This project presents another method of applying enamels – sifting – but it could be wet-packed as well. Project 4, *Awesome Blossoms,* is a good example of wet-packing flat surfaces. Sifting is a quick and fairly easy enamel application method, but wet-pack-

ing always gives you more control over your enamel, especially on small jewelry projects.

Prepare your work space for enameling, and preheat your kiln. Clean your silver with ammonia and a glass brush before you begin. Place a stack of clean paper (recycled is fine) on your work area.

Use a brush to paint undiluted Klyr-Fire onto the back of your piece **[7]**. Using the lightest shade of the enamel you plan to use on the front, place a small scoop of enamel into the sifter and gently sift an even layer of enamel onto your piece by running your fingernail up and down the twisted handle **[8]**. Carefully check the front for any stray grains; brush these away with a clean paintbrush or even your finger. The enamel should stick well to the Klyr-Fire, so turning it over to look shouldn't be a problem (see *Counter-enameling,* p. 39).

Place the piece, enamel side up, on a trivet and place it on a firing rack. Use a firing fork to carefully transfer the piece into the kiln. If using an UltraLite, use a low-profile trivet and a small spatula to move the piece in and out of the unit. Fire for 2 minutes, then remove and let the piece cool. It is not necessary for the enamel to have reached the smooth, glossy state. It just has to be fused enough

so it doesn't fall off when you turn the piece over. It will reach the glossy stage as you fire the rest of the enamels on the front.

Lightly mist the front of your piece with Klyr-Fire diluted 1:1 with distilled water **[9]**. Do not spray directly on the piece. Rather, spray above it and let the Klyr-Fire mist down onto it. Do not spray over your paper. You don't want any Klyr-Fire on the paper, or it will be hard to pour the excess enamel back into the jar later.

Begin sifting the various colors of enamel onto the front of the piece. Multiple colors can be used in one firing. You can create shading effects by overlapping colors **[10]**. Before firing, clear any stray enamel from the edges. Give it another light mist of Klyr-Fire to keep the enamel from dislodging when you move it.

After you sift on each color of enamel, curl the paper into a funnel shape to pour the excess back in the jar **[11]**. Use a fresh sheet or make sure the sheet is totally clean before moving on to the next color.

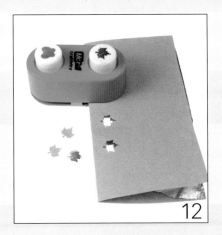

12

13

14

Holding just the edges, carefully move the piece to a clean trivet and place it on a firing rack. Fire for 2 minutes and then check the progress. If you are going to add another layer of enamel, you can take it out at the orange-peel stage and add another coat. Otherwise continue firing until it just reaches the smooth and glossy stage. Keep an eye on the enamel and take care not to over-fire.

Once the piece has cooled, you're ready to apply the gold foil. Fold a piece of paper in half and place the foil inside the crease. This helps make the foil easier to handle. Use a papercraft punch to punch out your foil shapes **[12]**. You also can use nail scissors to cut shapes. A pair of tweezers is helpful for separating the paper from the foil shapes.

Screen your 2020 Clear for Silver enamel to remove the fine particles (see *Preparing enamels,* p. 35). This step is necessary with the clear formulation to prevent the enamel from clouding and muting the shine of the gold foil.

Lightly mist your piece with Klyr-Fire. Position the foil on the piece and smooth it down **[13]**. The Klyr-Fire will keep it right where you want it. Once you have all the pieces in place, lightly mist it again, and sift on a layer of 2020 Clear for Silver enamel **[14]**. Fire the enamel for approximately 2 to 3 minutes, until it's smooth and glossy.

There is little finishing to be done on this piece since it's mostly covered with enamel. The edges can be polished a bit using Tri-M-Ite polishing papers and a polish cloth.

tip
Don't fall for faux foil! Typically what you find in craft stores may look like gold but rarely is. You want the real thing. Genuine 23K or 24K gold foil is obtained through jewelry suppliers in a variety of weights.

stringing the pendant

Cut two 26-in. (66cm) lengths of black silk cord. Fold one length in half and loop the folded end through one of the bails. Make a lark's head knot **[15]**. Repeat with the second cord on the other side.

To create an adjustable-length cord:
Treat each doubled section of cord as a single unit. Take the first cord and tie it in an over-hand knot around the second cord. Repeat, tying the second cord around the first cord. Knot the ends of the cords to prevent them from slipping through. Trim the excess.

15

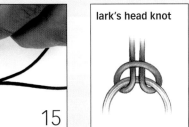

lark's head knot

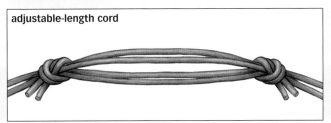

adjustable-length cord

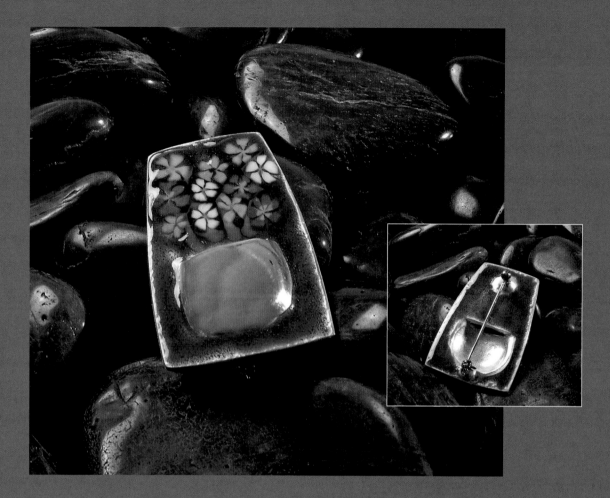

awesome blossoms

Pin with enamel floral wafers and threads

Enamel millefiori are made from long canes of enamel that have been cut into thin slices. In this project, you'll learn to use these beautiful little floral wafers along with enamel thread, which looks like thin pencil lead, to easily add intricate detail to your work. You'll also learn techniques such as attaching a pin-back finding and using cork clay to add dimension to metal clay.

For this project, I recommend using a low-fire clay with a low shrinkage ratio, such as Art Clay Silver 650 Low Fire. You need the pin parts to be the correct distance apart after the piece is fired, and the less shrinkage you have to deal with, the easier this is. Art Clay Silver screw-type pin findings provide a very professional finished look.

firing methods
Metal clay: programmable kiln or UltraLite
Enamel: programmable kiln

tools & supplies

Metal clay
- Metal clay tools (p. 11-13)
- Metal clay firing tools and equipment (p. 16-18)
- 20g ACS 650 Low Fire clay
- Metal clay syringe
- Metal clay paste
- Fine-silver screw-type pin finding (at least 35mm)
- Rubber-tipped clay shaper
- Cork clay

Enameling
- Enameling tools (p. 14-15)
- Enamel firing tools and equipment (p. 16-18)
- Tweezers
- Shallow cup
- *Thompson lead-free 80-mesh enamel (transparent):*
  2680 Prussian Blue
- Green enamel threads
- Enamel floral wafers

Finishing
- Two-part epoxy or E6000
- Toothpick

making the pin

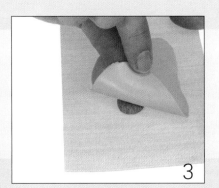

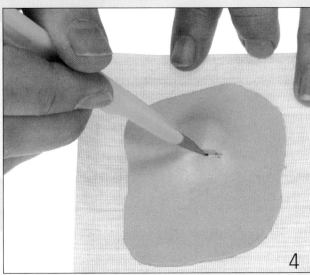

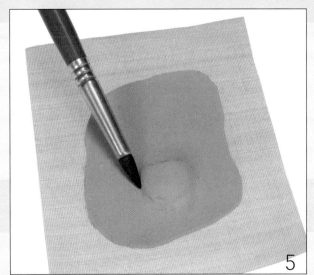

Mold about ½ teaspoon of the cork clay to create a flat-backed shallow dome, and cut off one end to create a flower pot shape **[1]**. Let it air dry overnight. Use 220-grit sandpaper to smooth and shape it after it dries.

Before getting out your clay, assemble the pin parts **[2]**. Position the joint and catch so the pin stem end just barely catches. The clay will shrink as it fires, causing the pin stem to move farther in. Measure the distance between the two base pieces. When you cut out your clay, you will need to make it long enough to accommodate the length of your pin stem.

Prepare your tools and work space. Roll the clay to an even thickness using the red slats (see *Rolling clay,* p. 22). Lay the clay over the cork form **[3]**, and cut it across the flat end to open the pot **[4]**. Use a rubber-tipped clay shaper to mold the clay around the cork form to shape the pot **[5]**. Use the cutter/scraper to cut out the shape of your pin **[6]**. A cutter/scraper can be bent gently to create smooth, curved cuts. Remember to check the length of the piece against your pin finding so you leave enough room to attach it later.

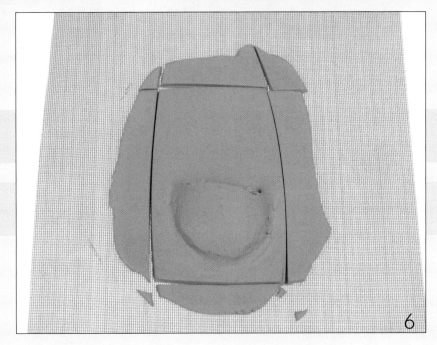

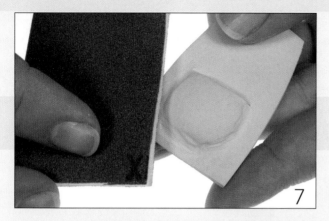

7

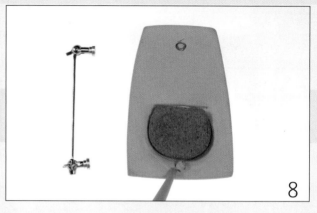

8

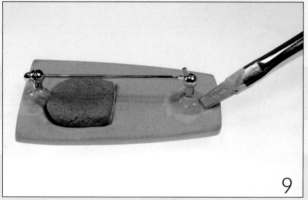

9

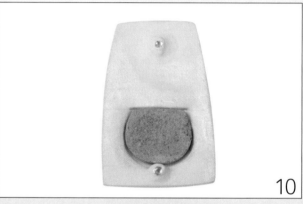

10

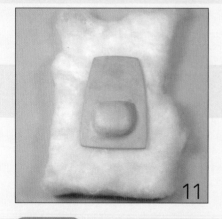

11

tip

Leave the pin and catch in place during all greenware finishing. If you remove them before you are done, stray clay dust or paste could get into the screw threads and prevent you from putting the piece back together after firing.

Dry the piece thoroughly and sand the greenware smooth. Use metal clay paste or syringe to fill any cracks or divots in the clay. Pay special attention to sanding and smoothing the pot portion of the pin in preparation for mirror finishing later **[7]**. You also can gently burnish the greenware with an agate burnisher to get an ultra-smooth finish (see *Mirror finishing,* p. 30).

Screw the hinge and catch into the base pieces. Place the catch and joint findings on the back of the greenware, adjusting the positions so the end of the pin stem is barely inside the catch. Use a pencil to mark where the base pieces need to go. For this piece, I placed the pin vertically, but if you are using a horizontal placement, you will want to position it towards the top of the piece with the catch opening facing down when closed (that way, the pin is more likely to stay in place should the catch come undone).

Place dots of metal clay syringe on the greenware at your pencil marks and press the base pieces into them **[8]**. Use a fine brush to apply paste or additional syringe material to smooth the base pieces into place and create a smooth, seamless connection **[9]**. A sponge-tip applicator is helpful for smoothing the connection. Let it dry completely.

Make sure there is no clay or paste on the cork before firing. You can use a needle file to scrape it off the cork. Before firing, remove the pin joint and catch, leaving the base pieces in place **[10]**. The pin and catch should not be fired. If firing in a programmable kiln, support the piece on a fiber blanket so the piece does not sag over the pin findings **[11]**. Do not use a fiber blanket if firing in an UltraLite. Fire with the findings down.

Since you are firing cork clay, you will need to ramp the kiln at a slightly slower speed. Before firing this piece, reset the ramp speed on your kiln to 4. If you are using an UltraLite, place it in the unit cold and let it come up to temperature slowly as the unit heats. Don't start your timing until the piece reaches a salmon-pink color. The cork clay will produce a small amount of smoke as it burns off (see *Firing metal clay,* p. 26).

After firing, brush and burnish. Use sandpaper and Tri-M-Ite to bring the edges and flower pot portion of the piece to a mirror shine. This may have to be touched up after enameling, but it's easier to get the lion's share of the finishing done before you apply the enamels.

enameling the pin

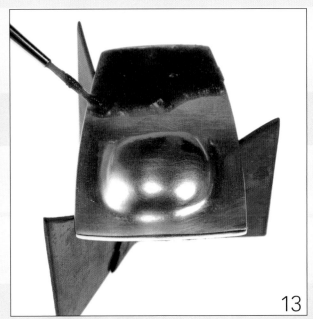

For this piece I recommend counter-enameling to prevent warping. It's flat and will have a fair amount of enamel covering most of the piece, so without counter-enamel, warping is likely. I also suggest enameling both sides at once.

Begin heating your kiln. Thoroughly clean the front and back of the piece with a glass brush and ammonia. Prepare your enamel for wet-packing (see *Preparing enamels,* p. 35). I recommend using the same color enamel on the back as you plan to use on the front. That way, if any stray enamel gets on the other side, it won't really matter. If you screened your enamels to improve clarity, the fines can be used for the back of the piece.

Apply the counter-enamel first. Add several drops of Klyr-Fire to the counter-enamel to help it stay in place when you turn the piece over. Place the piece face down on a trivet. Use a brush and a scribe to lay the enamel onto the back of the piece **[12]**. Take care that no enamel gets into the pin base holes. Since you will not be enameling the front of the flower pot, it's not necessary to enamel the back of it either. Just leave that part bare. Hold the edges of the piece and tap the edge with a metal tool to settle the enamel and bring the water to the surface. You can use a bit of paper towel to wick away the excess moisture.

Turn the piece over and place it back in the trivet face up. Apply the wet enamel to the front of the piece in the same way as you did for the back **[13]**. Be very careful to keep any

enamel off the flower-pot portion of the pin. Use your magnifying visor and a good task light. As long as you catch it before you fire the piece, you can easily use a clean brush to remove any stray grains. Hold the piece by the edges and tap it gently to settle the enamel and bring the water to the surface **[14]**. Wick away any excess water with a piece of paper towel.

Return it, face up, to the trivet and place it on a firing rack on top of the kiln to dry. Use a firing fork to transfer the entire rack, with the trivet, into your kiln. Fire for 2 to 3 minutes until glossy and smooth. Remove from the kiln and let cool. If any of your counter-enamel dropped off, you can fill it back in and refire it.

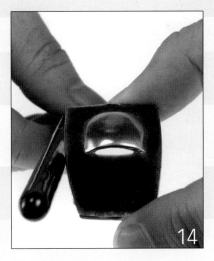

enameling the pin

15

Pour a little full-strength Klyr-Fire into a shallow cup. In this illustration I've used a glass votive, which is perfect for this. Use bentnose tweezers to dip the green enamel threads into the Klyr-Fire and lay them on the piece where you want the stems [15]. Place the piece back on the trivet on the firing rack and fire it for 2 minutes. Remove from the kiln and let cool. The threads should be fired in and relatively smooth at this point. Since the piece will be fired again, it doesn't matter if the stems are not completely flat yet.

Use the bentnose tweezers to dip the floral wafers in the Klyr-Fire and lay them on the piece to create the bouquet [16]. The wafers will spread out as they fire, so leave some room between them. They can be on top of the stems or next to them; it won't matter when it's through firing. Place the piece back in the kiln and check the piece at 2 minutes. If the floral wafers have not fused, put the piece back in for another minute. At this stage you will want all the enamel to reach a glossy and smooth state. You can fire the floral wafers until they are completely fused and flattened into the base layer of enamel, or you can leave them only partially fused, giving them a raised effect.

16

finishing the piece

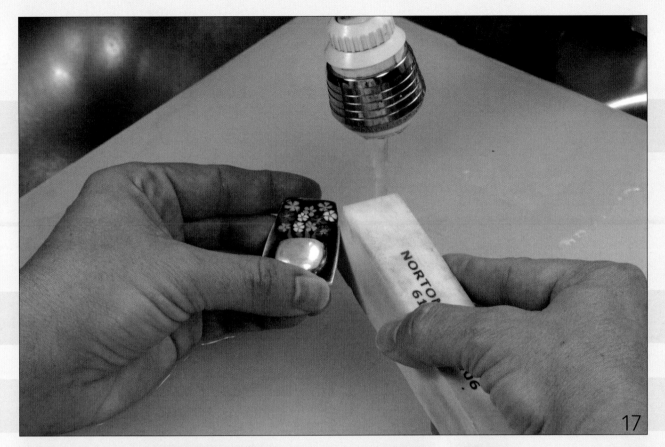

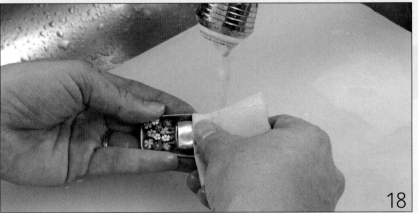

There should be enamel on the front and the back of the piece, but not on the edges. If there is any enamel on the edges you can grind it off using an alundum stone **[17]**. Always do any grinding or sanding with water. Use sandpaper and/or Tri-M-Ite polishing papers to polish the edges and take the flower pot to a mirror shine **[18]**.

Screw the pin parts into the base pieces to check the length and fit of the pin. If the pin is too long, trim it and file it back to a point. Remove the pin parts, place a drop of two-part epoxy or E6000 into the base holes using

a toothpick, and screw the parts back in **[19]**. Do one part at a time so the glue doesn't dry in one hole while you're working with the other. The pin portion has a small ear that should point down towards the piece when the pin is closed. This helps with the pin tension. Close and latch the pin while the glue dries.

screw-type pin finding

ear should point down

sink wide base into clay

let's go fly a kite!

Syringe-work cloisonné pendant

firing methods
Metal clay: programmable kiln, butane torch, or UltraLite
Enamel: programmable kiln or UltraLite

tools & supplies

Metal clay
- Metal clay tools (p. 11-13)
- Metal clay firing tools and equipment (p. 16-18)
- 10g metal clay
- Metal clay syringe with green tip
- Metal clay paste
- Large serving spoon
- Fine-silver bail back

Enameling
- Enameling tools (p. 14-15)
- Enamel firing tools and equipment (p. 16-18)
- *Thompson lead-free 80-mesh enamels (transparent):*
  2520 Aqua Blue
  2325 Gem Green
  2230 Lime Yellow

Finishing
- Beads
- Bead-stringing thread

Cloisonné is probably the most popular and well-known enameling technique. In traditional cloisonné, flat wires are bent to form cells that are then attached to a base piece. These cells are filled with enamel colors.

With metal clay, you can duplicate this look using a syringe with a medium or small tip. Because syringe work is round, not flat, like cloisonné wires, there are other factors you should consider. The enamel can undercut the syringe design, causing cracks or causing the syringe to lift from the base. To avoid problems, make sure the syringe is well-sealed to the base with paste. Use only a single layer of enamel and you shouldn't have any trouble with cracks.

making the kite

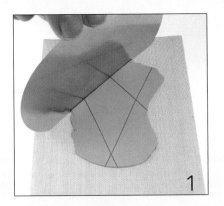

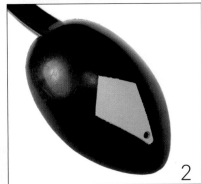

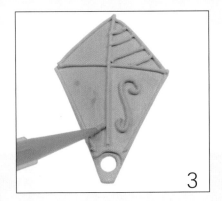

Roll clay to an even thickness using the blue or red slats (see *Rolling clay,* p. 22). Use a tissue blade or cutter/scraper to cut a kite shape **[1]**. Use a very small straw to cut a hole at the bottom of the kite shape, where you will later attach the tail. Lay the shape on the back of a large serving spoon to gently curve it **[2]**. Allow it to dry on the spoon.

After the piece is dry, sand and smooth any rough edges. Sand the points off the back side of the kite, rounding them slightly. This will make it more comfortable to wear after it's fired (see *Greenware finishing,* p. 23).

To help the syringe-design detailing stick better, dampen the surface of the piece with a brush and water. Use a syringe with a small or medium tip to apply the kite design **[3]**. After the syringe design has dried, use paste and a very small brush to reinforce the syringe connection with the base **[4]**. There should be no gaps or undercut areas. After the paste is dry, gently sand the top to slightly flatten the syringe work **[5]**. Remove the dust with a soft dusting brush.

tip
Applying syringe designs takes a bit of practice, but it's well worth the effort. Here are a few tips to help you along.

The syringe tip should touch the surface of your piece only to begin and end a line. Other than that, keep the tip well above your work (at least ½ in./13mm). Begin by touching the syringe at the start of a line to connect with the piece. Allow a length of clay to come out and hang suspended in the air, and then just lay it where you want it, rather than trying to force it into place with the tip. Don't pull on the syringe line, as this will cause it to become too thin or break. When you want to end, stop pressing the plunger on the syringe first, and then touch down where you want the line to end. If the beginning or end of the line has sharp points from the syringe tip, use a damp brush to gently pat them down.

making the pendant and bail

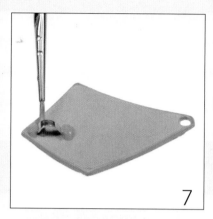

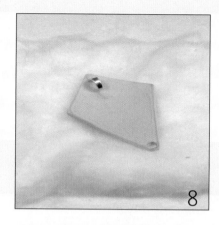

Attach a fine silver bail to the top back of the kite. Use a dot of syringe to fix the bail in place, then smooth it with paste **[6]**. After it's dry, reinforce the connection with additional paste **[7]**. The feet of the bail back should be covered.

If you are using a programmable kiln, support the domed shape of the kite with a fiber blanket **[8]** Do not use a fiber blanket if firing in an UltraLite; instead, fire the piece concave side up (bail up) for best results.

Fire, brush, and burnish. It will be difficult to use a hand burnisher inside the small cloisonné cells, so tumbling is better for this project. If you must hand burnish, try using a ball-tip burnisher (see *Firing clay*, p. 26, and *Postfire finishing*, p. 29).

enameling the kite

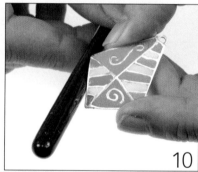

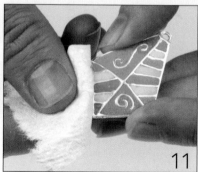

Prepare the silver for enameling by cleaning with a glass brush and ammonia. Prepare the enamels for wet-packing (see *Preparing enamels*, p. 35). Since this is a domed piece, you may find it helpful to add a drop of Klyr-Fire to the enamels to keep them from settling into the corners. Although I called for

transparent colors, this project would work equally well with opaque enamels, so you have lots of choices!

Begin laying the enamels into your pattern **[9]**. A magnifying visor will be very helpful for this (see *Wet-packing enamels*, p. 37).

Stop periodically and tap the edge of the piece to settle the enamel **[10]**. Draw off the excess water as you go along **[11]**. Be careful to keep the enamel off the syringe "wires."

When all the enamel has been applied, use your magnifying visor to make sure all the syringe wires are clear of enamel. Use a clean, damp brush to remove any excess enamel, or move it off the wire and into a cell [12]. Place the piece on a trivet and set it on a firing rack on your kiln to dry [13]. Once it is dry, fire the enamel until it is glossy and smooth (see *Firing enamels*, p. 40).

After the piece has cooled, it can be polished. Most of the silver finishing should have been done before the enamel was applied, so this step is just touch-up. The blue, pink, and

mint Tri-M-Ite papers are all that you should need. Work wet and concentrate on the silver, avoiding the enamel as much as possible [14]. Use a gentle touch to avoid putting any stress on the enamel. Finish up by buffing with a polish cloth.

tip

Because this is a domed piece and you will apply only one layer of enamel, counter-enameling should not be necessary.

finishing

For the tail, I prefer to use a fine beading thread rather than beading wire. The tail will not be supporting any significant weight or stress, so strength isn't a big issue, and the thread will give it more movement. The little bow beads make a great accent for this project, but a variety of other beads would work as well.

String one small bead onto the thread, fold the thread in half, and move the bead to the bottom of the fold [15].

String all but two or three of the remaining beads onto both threads. The first bead will keep them from sliding off the other end. For the last couple of beads, string them on just one of the ends of thread [16].

Loop the end through the hole in the bottom of the kite, and then thread it back through the top two beads.

Tie the two ends of the thread into a tight knot [17] and, if possible, tuck the knot into one of the beads, hiding it from view.

blue horizon

Three-dimensional enamel ring

firing methods
Metal clay: programmable kiln, butane torch, or UltraLite
Enamel: programmable kiln or UltraLite

It's surprisingly easy to add enamel to three-dimensional shapes. Rather than flowing down, as you might expect, enamel tends to stay where you put it. With the judicious use of Klyr-Fire and proper wet-packing technique, you can apply enamel to any number of shapes. This easy enameled ring is a great way to start working in new dimensions.

I highly recommend using Art Clay Silver 650 Slow Dry clay for this project. The low and consistent shrinkage makes it easy to properly size the ring, and the slow-dry clay gives you extra time to get it wrapped around the mandrel without cracking.

tools & supplies

Metal clay
- Metal clay tools (p. 11-13)
- Metal clay firing tools and equipment (p. 16-18)
- 10g Art Clay Silver 650 Slow Dry
- Art Clay syringe with green tip
- Art Clay paste
- Flat-band finger sizer
- Ring mandrel with stand
- Metal ring mandrel and mallet (optional)
- Clear tape

Enameling
- Enameling tools (p. 14-15)
- Enamel firing tools and equipment (p. 16-18)
- *Thompson lead-free 80-mesh enamels (transparent):*
  2520 Aqua Blue
  2530 Water Blue

making the silver ring

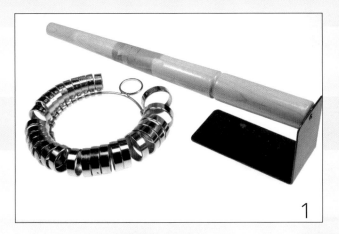

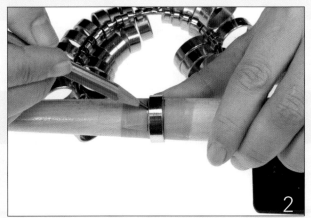

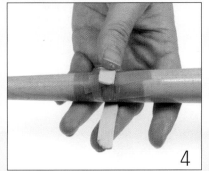

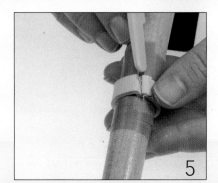

Begin by determining the size of your ring. This is a flat-band ring, and you should use a flat-band finger sizer to measure your finger. Go for a snug fit. If you find you are between sizes, use the smaller of the two. It's easier to make a tight ring a little bigger than it is to make a loose ring tighter. Once you have found your ring size, add two sizes. For example, if you have a size 7 finger, you will make a size 9 ring. That way, after the clay shrinks during firing, the finished ring should fit perfectly **[1]**.

Slide appropriate finger sizer onto the ring mandrel and mark the spot with a pencil. Wrap a strip of your nonstick work surface around the place where you will be making your ring and tape it in place. Remember, this will add thickness, so position it a bit towards the narrower end of the mandrel. Slide the finger sizer back onto the mandrel and mark along both sides with a pencil **[2]**. This is where you will make your ring.

Roll a long, narrow strip of clay using the red or blue slats. If this is your first ring, I suggest using the red slats (see *Rolling clay,* p. 22). Use one of the slats as a straightedge to cut a strip for the ring **[3]**.

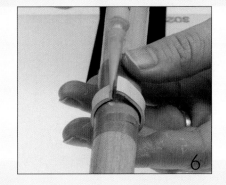

Wrap the piece around the ring mandrel at the spot you've marked **[4]**. I find it's helpful to cup my hand underneath to hold it in place while I position the top. The pieces should overlap. Use a cutter to cut through both pieces at an angle **[5]** and remove the trimmed bits. You may have to shave a hair more off one end. If you do, be sure to maintain the angle. Lay a line of syringe along one edge **[6]**, join the seam, and smooth it with a damp brush **[7]**.

tip

The directions for ring sizing for this project assume ACS 650 is being used. If you are using a different type of metal clay, please refer to the manufacturer's instructions for ring sizing.

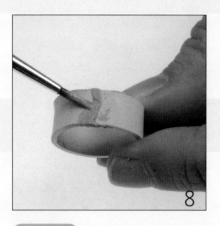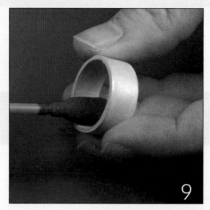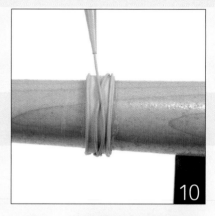

Enameling on Metal Clay

tip

To create an invisible seam, slightly overfill the seam on the inside as well as the outside, then sand it down after it's dry.

overfill

Allow the ring to dry on the mandrel. If you have a big dehydrator, the entire mandrel can go in; otherwise, let it air dry at least 24 hours.

Carefully remove the ring from the mandrel and reinforce the seam inside and out with syringe and/or paste [8]. For enameling, it's important the ring not have a thin spot at the seam as that can cause cracks in the enamel later on. The finished seam should be invisible both inside and out.

Sand and smooth the inside, outside, and edges of the ring. Sanding swabs make finishing the inside of a ring a breeze [9]. Bevel the edges slightly so they won't be sharp and uncomfortable when you wear the ring. Once the seam is invisible and the sanding is done, you are ready to apply your syringe design.

Run a damp paintbrush or sponge-tip applicator over the surface of the ring to slightly dampen the clay. This will help your syringe work stick better. Place the ring back on the ring mandrel to make it easier to turn while you apply your design [10]. Be sure to leave spaces in your pattern for the enamel. I find it's easiest to hold the syringe above the ring a half inch or so, rather than setting the tip on the ring. Allow the syringe clay to come out and then

lay it down on the ring. Maintain the position of the syringe tip above the ring, and turn the mandrel to move the design along.

After your syringe design is on, use a damp brush to gently pat it in to place. The goal is not to flatten the syringe work, but to make sure it's connected to the ring all the way around. Allow the syringe work to dry. Use a very fine paintbrush to apply clay paste to ensure the syringe clay is well connected to the ring at all points [11]. Use a magnifying visor for this step. You don't want any gaps where the enamel could slip underneath the syringe line.

After it's dry, feel your way around the ring looking for sharp ends. Lightly sand anything that sticks up. The ring should be smooth and comfortable to wear. Use a soft brush to dust it off.

Fire the ring. This project can be fired successfully in either a regular kiln or an UltraLite (see Firing metal clay, p. 26). Before doing any postfire finishing, check the roundness of your ring. If the ring is not round, place it on a metal ring mandrel and gently tap it back into shape using a rawhide or nylon mallet [12]. Brush and burnish. Tumbling is the best method for shining up this project.

enameling the ring

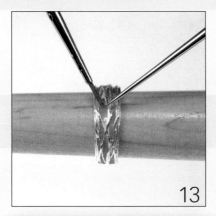

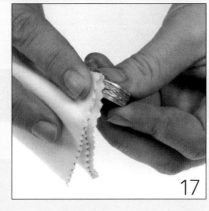

Rings take a lot of wear and tear. You'll want to add only a single layer of enamel for this project so the enamel will be protected by the raised syringe pattern.

Preheat your kiln for enameling. Clean the ring with ammonia and a glass brush. Rinse and dry. Prepare your enamels for wet-packing, adding a few drops of Klyr-Fire to each color (see *Preparing enamels,* p. 35).

Begin laying in your enamels using a very fine brush and a scribe **[13]**. You'll need to use a magnifying visor for this step. Be very careful not to get enamel on top of the syringe-work wires, only within the pattern on the flat band of the ring. You can hold your ring steady on the ring mandrel while you work. Be sure the mandrel is clean so you do not introduce any metal clay dust or other impurities into your enamels. Work on one side of the ring at a time, lightly tapping the enamel into place, and wicking away excess moisture before moving on to the next section.

When you're done applying the enamels, check the ring carefully while wearing a magnifying visor. Make sure you have enamel only where you want it. Use a clean brush to remove any unwanted enamel **[14]**. For this

project especially, it can be a time-consuming process, but it's worth the effort.

Lay the ring on its side on a sheet of mica on a firing rack **[15]** and place it on top of the kiln to dry. Fire for 2 minutes and then check it. If it's not yet glossy and smooth, put it back for another minute. Continue checking until the enamel is completely fired.

Once it's cooled, you can polish it up. Most of the finishing work was done before the enameling, so this should just be a touch-up. Use the finer grits of Tri-M-Ite (blue, pink, and mint) to brighten up the high points of the wires **[16]**. Follow up by buffing with a Sunshine cloth **[17]**. Do not use metal polishes as these will get down into the design and can be difficult to clean out properly.

here kitty kitty!

Paper-punch champlevé pendant

firing
methods
Metal clay:
programmable kiln
or UltraLite
Enamel:
programmable kiln

Champlevé involves using enamel to fill depressions in metal. Achieving fine detail like the silhouette of a tiny cat would be very exacting and difficult using traditional metalworking methods, but with metal clay paper or sheet and a paper punch, it's a snap!

When I show people this champlevé kitty sitting in a window, the reaction is pretty much a universal, "Oh! Isn't that cute!" Whether you end up with cute or classy will depend, in large part, on which craft punch you choose. Craft punches are available in a huge selection of designs. Imagine leaves falling across a field of yellow and orange or snowflakes drifting through a sea of blue. Explore the possibilities!

tools & supplies

Metal clay
- Metal clay tools (p. 11-13)
- Metal clay firing tools and equipment (p. 16-18)
- 15g metal clay
- Metal clay paste
- Metal clay paper/sheet
- Metal clay syringe with medium tip
- Craft punch (approx. ¾-1 in./19-25.5mm)
- Embossing tool or other stylus
- Paper
- Pencil
- Scissors
- Steel bench block and mallet (optional)

Enameling
- Enameling tools (p. 14-15)
- Enamel firing tools and equipment (p. 16-18)
- *Thompson lead-free 80-mesh enamels (transparent):*
  2510 Cascade Blue
  2520 Aqua Blue
  2530 Water Blue

Finishing
- Sterling silver snap-on bail

making the silver piece

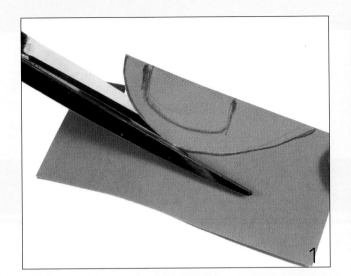

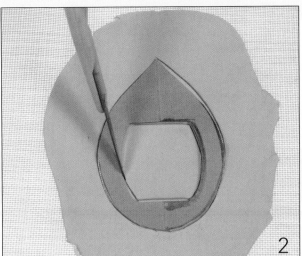

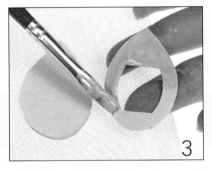

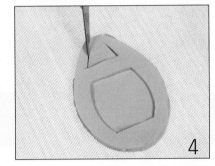

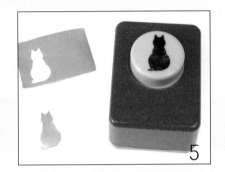

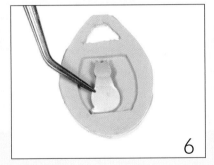

tip

To create a symmetrical shape, fold the paper in half when cutting out your pattern.

tip

When choosing clay and sheet for this project, be sure the two types have the same shrinkage rates.

Prepare your work space and tools. Decide on the shape of your piece and cut out a paper pattern including both the outer shape and the interior space you want to enamel [1]. Make sure you leave adequate space for any punched shapes you want to use.

For the most efficient use of your clay, it's easier if you roll out the top piece first, and then the base piece. Roll out all the clay using the green slats. Lay the pattern on the clay and cut out both the outside shape and the interior space [2]. Recondition the excess clay and roll it out again using the red or blue slats. Use the pattern again to cut out just the outside shape this time. Using a generous amount of paste, join the top piece to the bottom [3]. Smooth it to remove any air

bubbles. Use additional paste to seal any gaps between the top and the bottom layers. Cut a bail hole through both pieces at once [4].

Punch two matching shapes from the paper-type clay [5]. For this example I've used a cat punch, but any small craft punch will work. Use a generous amount of paste to affix one shape into your piece [6]. Use additional paste to stack the second shape on top of the first [7]. Make sure it aligns with the first shape exactly. The goal is to bring the punched shapes up to the level of the outer frame of the piece. The thickness of the paper-type clay will vary by brand. You may find you need an additional punched shape to bring it up high enough.

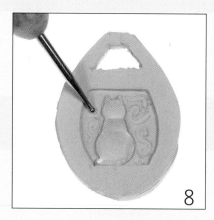

8

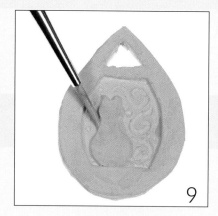

9

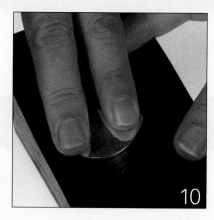

10

Use an embossing tool or stylus to create a background texture if desired **[8]**. If your clay has begun to dry at this point, you can brush on some water or a little metal clay paste, which will soften it enough to apply a texture.

Place the entire piece on a very flat surface and let it air dry. I don't recommend using a dehydrator or any other heated drying method for this project as it may cause it to warp.

Once the piece is dry, use paste and a fine-tip paintbrush to carefully seal the edges all the way around the interior space **[9]**. Pay special attention to the edges of the stacked piece. There should be no gaps, overhangs, or undercuts. The sides should be straight, smooth, and well-sealed to the base. Use a magnifying visor during this step. Any gaps could

cause cracks in your enamels later on. You may need to repeat this step several times to eliminate all the gaps. Use paste and/or syringe to fill and seal the outside edges of the piece as well.

Once all paste has dried, sand and smooth the greenware in preparation for mirror finishing. As a last step, use an agate burnisher to gently give the greenware the smoothest possible surface prior to firing (see *Mirror finishing,* p. 30).

Fire the pendant (see *Firing metal clay,* p. 26). If the piece warped during firing, you can flatten it by tapping it with a rawhide or nylon mallet on a steel bench block. Brush and burnish. I recommend using a tumbler for burnishing this project as it is very difficult

to get a hand burnisher into all the tight little spaces; however, a ball-tip agate burnisher should work if you can't use a tumbler.

Continue mirror finishing the piece. If you did a good job in the greenware stage, you should be able to begin with 600-grit sandpaper and work up from there **[10]**. Work through 600-, 1000-, and 1500-grit sandpapers before switching to Tri-M-Ite sheets. Use all the colors of Tri-M-Ite, working from coarse to fine **[11]**. Since there is no enamel on the piece yet, this can be done either wet or dry.

how to flatten a warped piece

If your piece warped as it was drying, you can flatten it out fairly easily. Place a very damp sponge inside a zip-top plastic bag. Lightly mist your piece with water and place it in the bag next to, but not touching, the sponge, and seal the bag closed. Let it sit overnight. The next day, when you remove the piece from the bag, you should be able to gently press it flat without cracking or breaking it. Place it between two flat objects such as ceramic tiles and allow it to finish drying. If you want, you can layer some nonstick sheets above and below the piece to protect it.

enameling the pendant

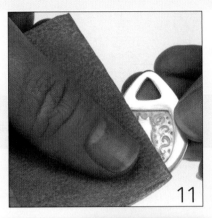

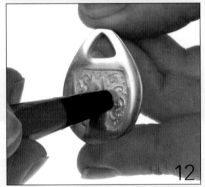

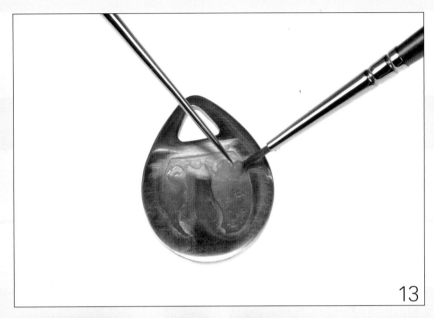

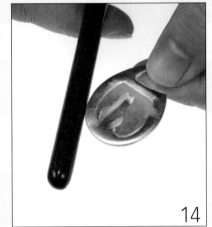

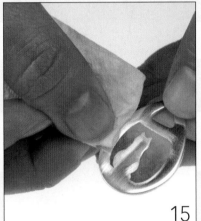

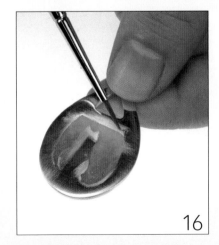

In this part of the process, we will fill the depression in the metal with several thin layers of enamel. Because the enamel can be thick by the time the layering is finished, and there are a lot of tight corners that can stress the enamel, counter-enameling will be necessary to prevent cracking. For this project, I've found it works best to fire the first layer on the front, then apply the counter-enamel, and then continue with the front.

Preheat the kiln. Clean the piece thoroughly with a glass brush and ammonia **[12]**. Rinse and dry. This step is especially important because of the pre-enamel sanding that was done. Any stray sanding grit can cloud and discolor the enamels. Take care to get into all the little nooks and crannies with the glass brush.

Prepare your enamels for wet-packing (see *Preparing enamels,* p. 35). Although it is listed as optional, I highly recommend screening your enamels for this project. You will be applying several layers of enamel to a significant depth. Minor clouding, which would not be particularly noticeable in a single layer of enamel, may spoil the effect significantly when working with multiple layers.

Using a very fine-tip paintbrush and a scribe, begin laying the enamels in the recessed area

of the piece **[13]**. Work in very thin layers. It will be tempting to try to pile in a lot of enamel all at once to save time, but this can result in bubbles and pits in your finished enamel. Also, you will have more control over your shading if you work thin. Start with your lightest color and use it over a third of the area. Switch to your medium color for the next third, and so on. Use your scribe to move the particles around where dark and light meet to blend the area. If the enamel does not want to settle easily, add more water.

Tap the edge of the piece lightly with a metal tool to settle the enamels **[14]**, and then use a bit of torn paper towel to wick away the excess moisture **[15]**. Use a good light and a magnifying visor to carefully check for any stray enamel that might have gotten onto the silver surfaces of the piece. Use a clean brush to brush them away or brush them back into the enameled portion of the piece **[16]**. If you

accidentally fire enamel onto the frame of the piece, you can use an alundum stone to remove it later, but this will cause scratches that will have to be sanded out. A little care at this stage will save you a lot of work later.

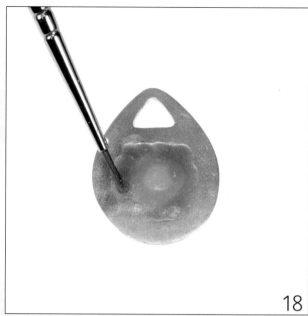

Set the piece on a clean trivet on a firing rack and place it on top of the kiln to dry **[17]**. The danger when firing multiple layers of enamel is over-firing, which can cause the enamel colors to darken and/or brownish areas to appear at the edges, where the enamel meets the silver. Fire for just 1½ to 2 minutes, until it is past the granulated stage but has not reached the orange-peel stage. It should not yet be glossy and smooth. If you reached the glossy stage, try a shorter firing time on the next firing. If you have a kiln with a window or peephole, you can watch the enamel to see when it reaches the orange-peel stage, and remove it at that point. Always wear kiln-appropriate safety glasses when looking into the kiln.

Allow the piece to cool and apply the counter-enamel to the back of the piece **[18].** You can be creative with the counter-enamel – it doesn't have to be all one color. Focus on the area behind the enameled area on the front. It isn't necessary to counter-enamel areas that will not have enamel on the other side. As with the enamel on the front, tap the edge to settle the enamel and wick away the excess moisture. While the enamel is damp, you can turn the piece over without disturbing it. Check the front carefully to make sure no stray grains of enamel have gotten onto the frame. Turn it back over, place it on a trivet, and let it dry. Fire to the orange-peel stage.

Now begin the next layer of enamel on the front. This time go a little farther across with the lighter shade of enamel, overlapping some of the medium color. Do the same with

the other colors. This overlapping will enhance the shading effect. Again, use the scribe to blend the enamels where they meet, and check carefully for stray enamel. Dry and fire to orange-peel stage. Continue in this fashion and with each firing, advance the lighter shades slightly over the darker. Ultimately, the enamel should be just slightly below the level of the frame. For your last firing, you want to fire it completely. Start with a 2-minute firing, but it may take longer. Check it often to avoid over-firing. Remove the piece from the kiln as soon as all the enamel is glossy and smooth.

It is possible to bring the enamel entirely level with the silver; however, this makes the final finishing much more complicated. By having the enamel just slightly recessed you will be able to easily mirror-finish your silver while retaining the glossy shine on your enamel.

finishing the piece

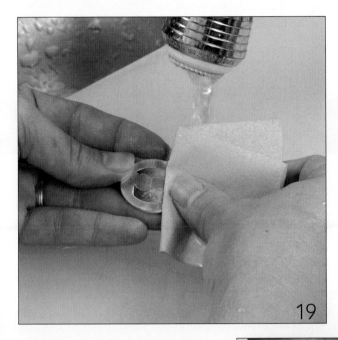

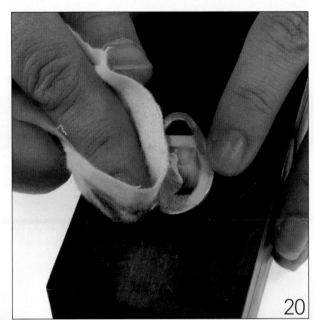

Remember, you always need to work wet when grinding or sanding pieces containing enamels. I recommend using a rubber block and working at a sink. I run a slow stream of water over the block as I work, keeping everything cool and wet. All sandpapers should be of the "wet/dry" variety.

If you see any stray enamel, you can grind it off with an alundum stone, in which case you will need to repeat all the mirror-finishing steps to get rid of the scratches. If you were careful, however, and no enamel got on the frame, bringing the silver back to a mirror shine should be fairly quick and easy. You should be able to polish it up using just the blue, pink, and mint Tri-M-Ite papers **[19]**. Take care to avoid sanding or polishing the enamel. Since you left it recessed a bit, this shouldn't be hard. Also polish the sides and any exposed areas on the back of the piece as you go along. Buff the silver to final polish with metal polish and a soft flannel cloth **[20]**. Attach the sterling silver snap-on bail **[21]**.

tip
Snap-on bails are available from silver-finding suppliers.

bayou bracelet

Torch-fired basse-taille beads

firing methods
Metal clay: programmable kiln, butane torch, or UltraLite
Enamel: propane torch

My introduction to enameling was with torch-fired beads. I had been working on copper for some time and was ready to try silver. At the time I lacked any silversmithing skills and quickly discovered that fine-silver tubing was nearly impossible to find. When I heard about metal clay, it seemed the perfect solution. I could make my own tubes and, taking it one step further, I could texture and pattern them to create wonderful basse-taille beads.

Basse-taille is French for "low-cut" or bas relief. In this technique, a low relief pattern is covered entirely with a single color of transparent enamel. Where the pattern cuts deep, the enamel is a darker color, and where it's shallow, the color is lighter. Traditionally, the relief pattern would be etched, but with metal clay you can easily get the same results with a texture plate.

tools & supplies

Metal clay
- Metal clay tools (p. 11-13)
- 4g metal clay per bead
- Metal clay paste
- 4 cocktail straws, cut in half
- Texture plates or stamps
- Firing brick
- Butane torch
- Timer

Enameling
- Enameling tools (p. 14-15)
- Propane torch (BernzO-matic TS4000 recommended)
- Propane cylinder, 400g (14.1 oz)
- Torch holder
- 6-in. (15.2mm) slip-joint pliers
- Flathead screwdriver
- Mandrel handle
- ¼-in. (6.5mm) mandrel tip
- Index or business card
- Small spoons
- 8-in. (20.3cm) ceramic tile

- 12-in (30.5cm) ceramic tile
- Lazy susan or banding wheel
- Large slotted spoon or wire mesh
- Slow cooker
- Vermiculite
- Safety glasses
- Dust mask
- *Thompson lead-free 80-mesh enamels (transparent):*
  2230 Lime Yellow
  2520 Aqua Blue
  2420 Sea Green

Finishing
- .014 bead-stringing wire
- Silver crimp tubes
- Clasp
- Accent beads
- Wire cutters
- Crimping pliers

creating the bead tubes

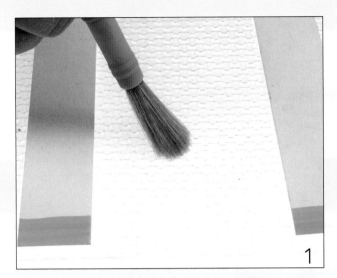

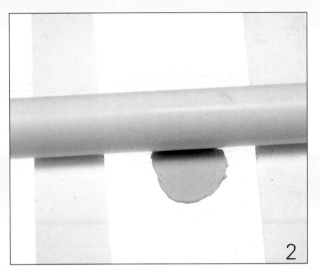

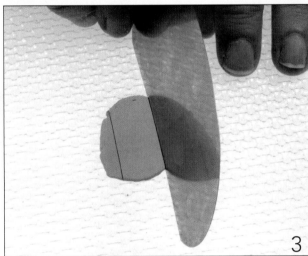

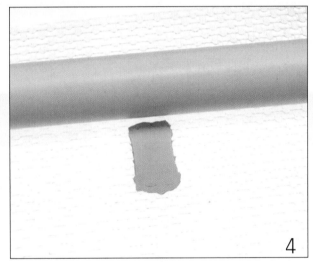

Prepare your work space and tools. Your texture sheet needs to be lightly coated with olive oil. Tap the flat end of a stencil brush on a sponge saturated with olive oil, and then brush the texture sheet **[1]**. Oil should not pool in your texture.

Use the green slats to roll out the clay. Lay the slats directly on the texture sheet **[2]** and roll to an even thickness. Remove the slats and, leaving the clay on the texture sheet,

use a cutter/scraper to trim the piece **[3]**. The cutter/scraper will cut the clay easily without damaging the texture sheet. Keeping the clay on the texture sheet, roll the short ends of the clay to taper them **[4]**. This will allow you to wrap the clay around the straw twice without it getting too bulky. The finished tube should be a fairly even thickness all the way around when it's done.

tip

Plastic texture sheets are effectively two-sided. You get a positive image on one side and a negative on the other. Either side will work fine, but you'll want to decide which you like best. I suggest pressing a bit of polymer clay into each side to see the results before you roll out your metal clay.

tip

Vermiculite is a soil lightener. Look for it at a garden supply store.

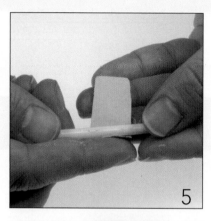

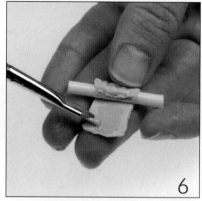

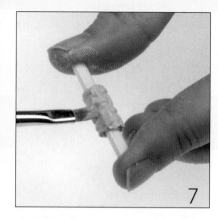

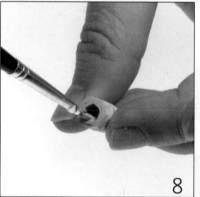

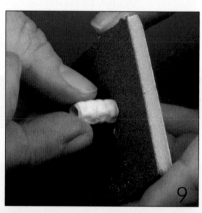

tip

Use a handheld butane torch to fire the beads one at a time. I don't recommend a propane torch for this step because it's harder to control and it's too easy to melt the silver.

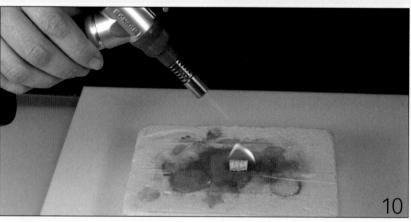

Remove the clay from the texture sheet. Dampen one end of the clay and make a complete wrap around a straw **[5]**. I suggest using a cocktail straw because larger drinking straws make the hole too big for the clay to fit snugly on the enameling mandrel you'll use later in this project. Apply a thick, generous amount of paste to the remainder of the clay strip and make a second wrap over the first **[6]**. Use a brush to smooth the seam **[7]**.

Repeat to make 5 or 6 more beads, and set them aside to dry. Remove the plastic straws. Sometimes it takes longer for the clay to dry where it's in contact with plastic, so give them

additional drying time after you remove the straw. Greenware finishing is fairly simple for beads. Use paste or syringe to fill any gaps or seams **[8]**. Once the bead is completely dry, just sand the ends **[9]**.

Fire the beads one at a time. Place a bead on the firing brick. Light the butane torch, and use a gentle sweeping motion to begin heating the bead. The piece will flame up **[10]**. That's just the binder media burning off and is normal. Continue heating the piece until it takes on a light salmon-pink color. Once it reaches this color, start timing for 2 to 3 minutes. Hold the piece at the pink color

for the entire time. If the bead starts turning a brighter orange color, pull the torch back. It takes only a moment for it to go from orange to melted. Remember to keep moving the flame around the piece. When the time is up, turn off the torch and use tweezers to move the bead off the brick to cool. Fire each bead this way.

Brush and burnish the beads. Tumbling is always the best way to burnish silver to be enameled, especially heavily textured, three-dimensional pieces like these tube beads.

enameling the beads

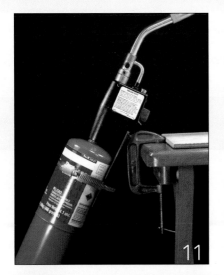

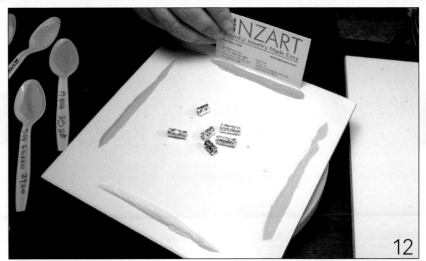

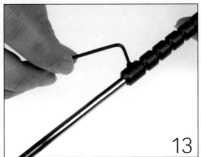

Torch-firing enamel beads is quite different than the other types of enameling presented in this book. It is not necessary to clean the silver with a glass brush prior to enameling. The torch flame will burn off any impurities before you start applying the enamel.

These first few steps involve setting up your work space. Carefully review the sidebar on bead-making safety before you begin.

Begin heating the vermiculite 30 minutes prior to making the beads. A small slow cooker works great for this.

The torch head screws directly onto the top of the propane cylinder. Use a torch holder to tightly attach the torch and cylinder to the edge of the table **[11]**. Place the large ceramic tile (or a cookie sheet) directly under the torch.

Place the smaller tile on top of the lazy susan. Use a small spoon to put the enamel on the tile, and use an index card or business card to push the enamel into a line along one edge of the tile **[12]**. You can lay out other colors along the other edges of the tile if you like. The lazy susan will allow you to turn the tile as needed to use the various colors.

bead-making safety

- **Handle propane equipment with caution. Follow the manufacturer's instructions for safe handling and storage.**

- **Always wear safety goggles when making glass beads. Didymium or Ace safety glasses reduce eyestrain from looking at the torch flame, and will protect your eyes should a bit of enamel pop off while you're firing it.**

- **Keep a fire extinguisher on hand when you work with an open flame. Keep the area in front of the torch clear of flammables, and work over a non-flammable surface. Ceramic tiles or a metal cookie sheet work great.**

- **Work in a well-ventilated area. If the room you're working in is small, place a box fan in a window blowing out.**

- **Tie back long hair, and wear close-fitting cotton clothing. Long pants and closed-toe shoes are recommended.**

- **Wear a dust mask whenever sifting or pouring vermiculite.**

Place a ¼-in. (6.5mm) mandrel tip in the mandrel handle and tighten the set screw **[13]**. Place the mandrel and pliers directly on your 12-in. tile. They will be very hot once you start working, so placing them on the tile will protect your table.

tip

I get my slow cookers from thrift stores and garage sales, and rarely pay more than a few dollars each.

14

15

16

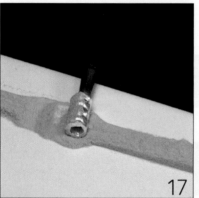

17

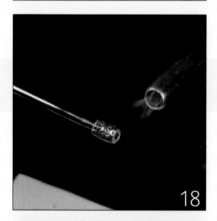

18

19

Place the bead on the mandrel tip and tighten it down **[14]**. The silver is soft, so to hold the bead in place without marring the pattern, you'll need to use your fingers. After the bead is on the mandrel, you can tighten it further a couple of ways. You can tap the end of the bead with the flat side, not the gripping teeth, of the pliers **[15]**. Also, you can heat it a bit in the torch flame and then press it down on your tile **[16]**. Both these methods should wedge the bead on the mandrel tip a bit tighter.

Heat the bead in the torch flame until it's just faintly pink. DO NOT get it red hot as it will melt. Roll the hot bead in your powdered enamel **[17]** and return it to the torch flame to fuse it on **[18]**. You need to reach only the orange-peel stage at first. Repeat this step three or four times, adding layers of enamel

until it is as thick as you want. You don't want to make it too thick, since that will obscure the pattern on your bead. Fire to the glossy and smooth stage on the very last layer.

Use the pliers to push the bead off the mandrel and into the hot vermiculite **[19]**. Once you have made all the beads you want, turn off the slow cooker and allow it to cool completely before sifting out the beads.

safety note

Using your fingers to hold the bead is best, so be sure your mandrel tip is completely cool to avoid burning yourself. You can quickly cool a hot tip by dunking it in a glass of water. This may shorten the life expectancy of your mandrel tip somewhat, but they are not expensive and it's better than singed fingers. If you are going to be doing several beads in one session, have two mandrels set up and alternate between them so each has time to cool down between beads.

finishing the beads

tip

Bracelets endure a lot of wear and tear. Next to rings, a bracelet probably takes the most abuse of any jewelry you're likely to wear, so you'll need to design it to stand up to stress. I recommend using Soft Touch .014 beading wire because it's strong and durable, and yet has the drape and flow of a softer stringing thread. For the best quality, use only sterling silver crimp tubes, never base metal.

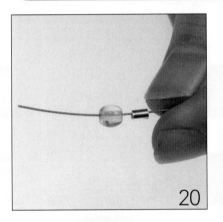

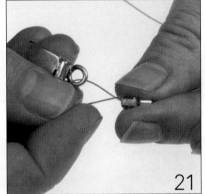

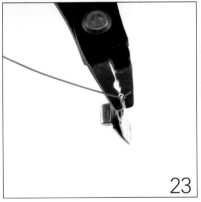

Very little finishing is needed for these pretty little beads. If you like, you can polish up the ends a bit, but that's really all.

Thread a silver crimp tube, followed by a very small fire-polished bead **[20]**. The bead helps reduce stress on the wire at the point where it joins the clasp. Thread the wire end through the clasp and back through the bead and crimp tube **[21]**.

Use a pair of crimping pliers to close the crimp tube. This is a two-part procedure. Use the back portion of the pliers to place a dent in the tube, keeping a wire to either side **[22]**.

Turn the tube 90° and use the front part of the pliers to fold and compress the crimp **[23]**. This is a very sturdy connection. No additional flattening is required. Trim the excess wire **[24]**. Continue stringing beads on the wire until the bracelet is the desired length.

String and secure the other half of the clasp using the same crimping procedure you used on the first end **[25]**. I used a purchased clasp for this example, but you could make a clasp out of metal clay if you wanted.

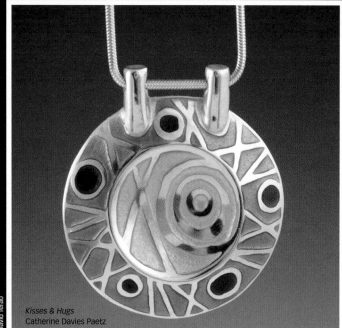

Photo: David Terao

Kisses & Hugs
Catherine Davies Paetz

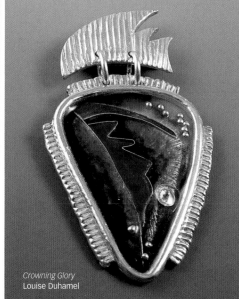

Crowning Glory
Louise Duhamel

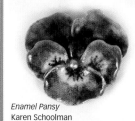

Enamel Pansy
Karen Schoolman

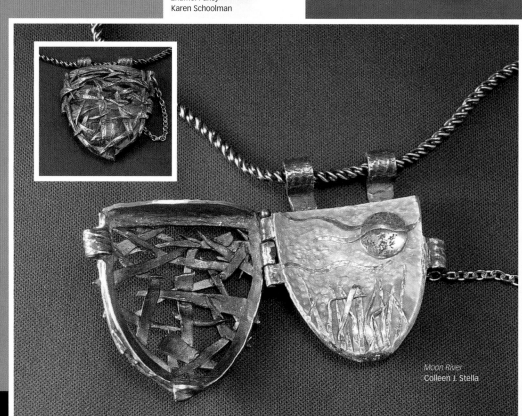

Moon River
Colleen J. Stella

For Naomi
M. Sue Way

Not Just a Clay Heart
Karen L. Cohen

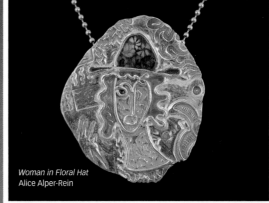

Woman in Floral Hat
Alice Alper-Rein

Fenji
Kate Qualley Peterson

Blue Spiral
Kathy Davis

Blue Tide
Joanne S Conant

Morning Glory Leaves
Olivia Competente

Photo: Todd Lista

Aqua Flower
Angela Foreman

Make a Wish
Pam East

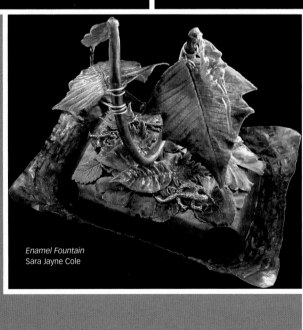

Enamel Fountain
Sara Jayne Cole

Monarch Butterfly
Olivia Competente

Southwest Flower Power
Janet Bocciardi

Dogwood
Nancy Duden

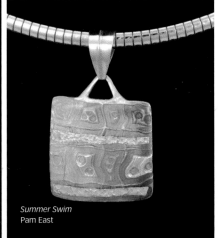

Summer Swim
Pam East

Folkart Sunburst
Pam East

Soaring into Happiness
Robin Weinrich

Geometry Glass
Catherine Davies Paetz

Enamel troubleshooting

Now that you've had a chance to try your hand at enameling, here are answers to common problems you may have encountered.

I don't like the way my piece turned out. How do I get the enamel off?
For best results, fire your enamels onto a test piece so you know what to expect. But if you're determined to start over, see the technique on p. 45.

My enamel cracked.
Several different things can cause cracks in the enamel. Before attempting to fix the enamel by refiring, be sure to clean it well with the glass brush and ammonia. Any oils or impurities in the crack can prevent it from healing properly.

The following questions should help you narrow down the problem.

Did you counter-enamel the piece?
If you didn't, this is your first line of defense. Lack of counter-enamel is the most common cause of cracks. It's not too late! Clean the enamel on the front with a glass brush and ammonia, apply your counter-enamel, and refire the piece. As the counter enamel fuses, the cracks on the front of the piece will heal. Thoroughly cleaning the front is important; any oils or dirt in the crack can prevent it from healing properly.

Is this a stacked piece like the cat champlevé on p. 76?
When creating a two-layer piece with cutouts for enamel, the joint between the layers may not be sealed. In this case, enamel can get into the gap between the two, causing the enamel to crack. Fill the joint with paste before you fire the metal clay. Make sure you use enough to get a good seal. [a]

Is this a syringe piece like the kite pendant on p. 68?
When using syringe to create cells, the enamel can undercut the syringe. This can result in two problems: cracks in the enamel and the syringe work lifting from the base. Be sure the base of the syringe work is well-sealed with paste. Don't try to add more than one or two thin layers of enamel unless you have added enough paste to the base of the syringe work to make the sides flat instead of round. [b]

Is this a stamped image like the quick earrings on p. 48?
Rubber-stamped images have sloped sides. The change in depth can cause cracks around the edge. This usually isn't a problem if you apply only one layer of enamel, but it becomes more of an issue if you choose to fill the image to the top. If you want to fill it all the way, prepare the piece in the greenware stage by running a file or carving tool gently around the edges of the image to create a straight-sided area to be filled. [c]

I scratched the enamel.
Fortunately, it's pretty easy to get scratches out. You just need to flash-fire the piece. Flash-firing means firing at a high temperature for a short period of time. The goal is to melt just the very top layer of enamel, getting rid of the scratch, without re-fusing the enamel all the way through. It is very important to clean the enamel thoroughly with ammonia and a glass brush before refiring. Any grit from sanding, oils from your fingers, or polishing compounds can affect the enamel and must be removed. Set the kiln to 1575°F (857°C). Fire for 45 seconds to 1 minute, checking it after 45 seconds. You can always put it back if the scratch doesn't disappear, but you don't want to over-fire it, so check it often.

After it cools, check to see if cleaning with the glass brush put any scratches into the silver. You should be able to buff these out fairly easily without scratching the enamel again by using just wet pink and mint Tri-M-Ite papers. Try to stay on the silver.

My enamel has pits in it.
It's possible you did not allow the enamel to dry completely before putting it into the kiln. Placing wet enamel in the kiln will cause the water to instantly convert to steam, often blowing the enamel out of the way in the process. This will result in pits and enamel scattered onto other portions of the piece.

Sometimes it's possible to repair the damage. Use an alundum stone to grind off any enamel that splattered where it didn't belong. Use a diamond bur on a rotary tool or flex shaft to grind out the pit. Clean the area thoroughly with a glass brush and ammonia. Wet-pack a bit of new enamel into the hole and refire it. Be sure to let it dry before refiring!

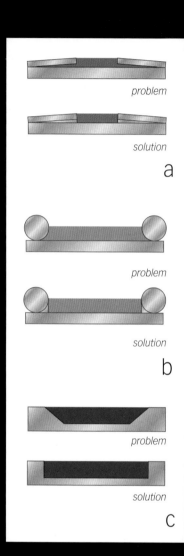

problem

solution

a

problem

solution

b

problem

solution

c

My enamel has bubbles in it.

Truthfully, nearly all enamels will have some bubbles in them. Usually these bubbles are small enough not to be particularly noticeable to the naked eye. Once in a while, however, you may get a larger bubble trapped beneath the surface. When this happens it may be that you applied the enamel too thickly for a single layer. Too much enamel at one time can leave air pockets underneath that become trapped bubbles after firing.

My transparent enamel came out cloudy.

Enamels contain very fine particles that can cause cloudiness after they are fired. You need to wash or screen the enamel before using it to remove these fine particles (see *Preparing enamels,* p. 35).

The enamel color became dark or brownish after firing.

There are two possibilities here. One is over-firing. If you fire the enamels too long or in too hot a kiln, they may darken or turn brown. To prevent over-firing, avoid firing at higher-than-recommended temperatures, and avoid firing for longer than it takes to fuse the enamel.

The second possibility is that you chose a color that reacts with silver. Some colors, such as red, yellow, pink, and orange, react when fired on silver and turn a brownish color. Be sure to test your colors before using them on your piece (see *Choosing enamels,* p. 33).

The enamel color changed dramatically after firing.

Again, there are two possibilities. Most likely you chose a color that reacts with silver (see *Choosing enamels,* p. 33). Another possibility is that the color change is normal. Some colors do not reach their full color potential until you fire them. They may appear pale or even white in the jar, but change to much stronger colors after they are fired. As always, test your enamels first!

I've fired to the glossy and smooth stage, but the enamel still shows ripples, lumps, or waves.

You did not settle the enamel properly before firing. Enamel is not a liquid and will not spread out during firing to fill low spots. It tends to stay right where you put it. If it's not level before you fire it, it won't be level after you fire it. Before firing, while it's still quite wet, tap the piece to settle the enamel (see *Wet-packing enamels,* p. 37).

I tried to enamel the silver earrings Aunt Betsy gave me, but all the enamel chipped off!

Most silver jewelry is made of sterling silver, not fine silver. Sterling silver, often marked 925, is 92.5% silver, 7.5% copper. Fine silver, like metal clay after firing, is 99.9% pure silver. Sterling silver cannot be enameled directly. It must first go through a process called depletion gilding.

To depletion-gild sterling silver, heat it until it darkens (using a torch or in a kiln) and then put it in a pickle solution to remove the oxidation. Repeat this process over and over until the metal appears whitish and does not darken when heated. At this point, all the copper has been refined out of the surface, leaving a thin skin of fine silver that can be successfully enameled.

resources

Recommended reading

The Art of Fine Enameling
by Karen L. Cohen

The Art of Enameling
by Linda Darty

Art Clay Silver & Gold
by Jackie Truty

Thompson Enamel Workbook
by Woodrow Carpenter, Bill Helwig, and Tom Ellis (Thompson Enamel, Inc.)

Classes and other educational resources; access to kilns
The Enamelist Society
enamelistsociety.org

Metal clay and enameling supplies
Pinzart, Inc.
(888) 335-9884
pinzart.com
My company, Pinzart, carries a full line of Art Clay Silver, metal clay tools, enameling tools, lead-free enamels, kilns and firing tools, and other jewelry craft tools and supplies. Although many of the supplies you'll need are fairly easy to locate, we sell some specialty supplies that may be a little difficult to find, such as the color-keyed graduated slat set, rubber blocks, Tri-M-Ite polishing papers, ultra-fine sponge-backed sanding pads, enamel floral wafers, and enamel threads.

Enamelwork Supply Co.
(800) 596-3257
ewsco@comcast.net
Leaded enamels, enameling tools and supplies

Tumblers
Lortone, Inc.
(425) 493-1600
lortone.com
Lortone is a tumbler manufacturer. The Lortone Web site includes a dealer directory.

Paintbrushes, stamps, clay tools, jewelry tools and other art supplies
Check your local art or craft supply store for these, or try an online retailer.

Rubber stamps
Rubber Nature ArtStamps
(262) 694-4058
rubbernature.com
All rubber stamps and rubber texture mats used in this book were designed and produced by Sandi Obertin of Rubber Nature ArtStamps.

Pam East is an enamelist and a certified Master Instructor in Art Clay Silver. She has written numerous articles for such magazines as *Lapidary Journal, Art Jewelry* magazine, *Glass on Metal,* and *Step-by-Step Beads.* Her video, "Enamel Bead Making," has received high praise in reviews. She has appeared on the *Carol Duvall Show* on HGTV, and also on *Jewelry Making* on the DIY Network. In 1997, Pam started Pinzart, her web-based store for enameling and metal clay tools and supplies. Born and raised in Southern California, Pam now resides in Alpharetta, Ga., with her husband, daughter, two cats, and Ferrari the Wonder Dog.

Pam says: "My philosophy can probably best be summed up as 'share the joy.' I love working with metal clay and enamels, and there's nothing I enjoy more than sharing my enthusiasm with my students and customers. Fun, I have found, is contagious. In my teaching, articles, and appearances, I have always worked toward making these art forms as accessible as possible to a wide audience. Even while maintaining a high standard of excellence, making beautiful jewelry need not be difficult or expensive."

Acknowledgments

I would like to express my sincere gratitude to the many people who have helped and advised me over the course of writing this book. Woodrow Carpenter of Thompson Enamel, for his patience, support, and over half a century of enameling expertise; Jackie Truty, Linda Michel, and Lorrene Davis for their comprehensive knowledge of metal clay and their willingness to share; Michelle Stewart for holding everything together while I was out of my mind; Dela Coward for helping me figure out my fancy new camera and how to take a decent process shot; my mother, Shirley Levinson, the professional nitpicker, for proofreading endless rounds of rewrites; my sisters, Jody Levinson and Donna Simon, for creative consulting and listening to me whine; my dad, Sandy Levinson, just for being there; and all my wonderful students who are a never-ending source of inspiration for me. Special thanks to Mary Lamberts and Lynn Ann Seeger, whose class projects inspired two of the projects in this book.

And most of all I want to thank my wonderful family, Steve and Katy East. Without their support, encouragement, and a willingness to fend for themselves for dinner, this book would not have been possible. I love you!